D1561687

Easy Spanish Phrase Book

1,000+ Common Phrases for Beginners and Travelers in Spain and Latin America

Also available:

Spanish Short Stories for Beginners (https://geni.us/ spanishbookbeginner)

Spanish Grammar for Beginners (https://geni.us/ spanishgrambeg)

For more products by My Daily Spanish, please visit:

https://store.mydailyspanish.com/

TABLE OF CONTENTS

INTRODUCTION

Whether you are planning to take a trip or trying to kick-start your lessons in Spanish, you've picked the right book to help you out.

This phrasebook aims to make your traveling experience in Spanish-speaking destinations as smooth as possible by giving you all the phrases and vocabulary you need to communicate in Spanish in a simple way.

This is not a book that will teach you Spanish. But it is a great guide to help you navigate all kinds of scenarios during your travel: from the moment you arrive at the airport, to getting around and doing touristy activities, to the more serious ones such as facing untoward events and emergencies.

This is a book that will make you feel confident to encounter any kind of scenario during your travels. Plus, it has bonus materials that will equip you with what you need to make the most of your vacation.

Here's what you'll find inside:

- **1,000+ Spanish words and expressions with English translations.** It includes an easy phonetic pronunciation guide.
- **Audio** to help you practice your listening and pronunciation skills in Spanish.
- **A menu reader to help you order the right food.** It contains food vocabulary and Spanish dishes translated from Spanish to English.
- **A pronunciation guide.**

Aside from tourists, this book would also benefit those who wish to give a boost to their Spanish language lessons. If you are a beginner level learner or you have previously studied

Spanish before but would like to review some basic phrases, this book is also great for you.

I hope you'll enjoy this book.

Gracias. Thank you,

My Daily Spanish Team

ADVICE ON HOW TO USE THIS BOOK EFFECTIVELY

Take this book with you during your travels in Spain and see how your level of confidence will greatly improve.

This book is arranged according to themes to make searching easier for you. Whatever scenario you find yourself in, just flip over to that page and take a look at the list of phrases. The first column contains the Spanish phrase, the second column is for the English translation of the phrase, and the third column is the easy phonetic pronunciation guide. Note that in the pronunciation guide, the stressed syllable is marked with a " ' " at the beginning of that syllable! For example, "'grah-see-ahs" signifies that the stress falls on the "grah."

If you wish to practice the correct pronunciation or train your ears to listen to Spanish as spoken by native speakers, you can also listen to the audio material which is offered for free with this book.

On the last page of this book (Page 126), you will find the link for downloading the audio files that accompany this book. Save the files onto any device and listen to them anywhere.

Important! The link to download the Audio Files is available at the end of this book. (Page 126)

PART 1 – FRASES ESENCIALES / ESSENTIAL PHRASES

CHAPTER 1: LOS BÁSICOS DEL ESPAÑOL / THE SPANISH BASICS

Listen to Track 1

Spanish	English	Pronunciation
Hola	*Hi*	'oh-lah
Sí	*Yes*	see
No	*No*	noh
Por favor	*Please*	'pohr fah-'bvohr
Mucho gusto.	*Nice to meet you.*	'mooh-choh 'goohs-toh
Me llamo...	*My name is...*	meh 'yah-moh
¿Cómo te llamas? (*informal*) / ¿Cómo se llama Usted? (*formal*)	*What's your name?*	'koh-moh teh 'yah-mahs /'koh-moh seh 'yah-mah oohs-'tehd
Somos de... Inglaterra/ Canadá/ los Estados Unidos.	*We're from... England/ Canada/the USA.*	'soh-mohs deh... een-glah-'teh-rrah/kah-nah-'dah/lohs ehs-'tah-dohs ooh-'nee-dos
Soy de...	*I'm from...*	'soh-ee deh
Gracias.	*Thank you.*	'grah-see-ahs
Muchas gracias.	*Thank you very much.*	'mooh-chahs 'grah-see-ahs
No, gracias.	*No, thanks.*	noh, 'grah-see-ahs

Listen to Track 2

No entiendo.	*I don't understand.*	noh ehn-tee-ˈehn-doh
No hablo español.	*I don't speak Spanish.*	noh ˈhah-bvloh ehs-pah-ˈnyohl
¿Hablas inglés? (*informal*) / ¿Habla Usted inglés? (*formal*)	*Do you speak English?*	ˈah-bvlahs een-ˈglehs / ˈah-bvlah ooh-ˈstehd een-ˈglehs
Disculpe.	*Excuse me.*	dee-ˈskoohl-peh
¿Dónde está el baño?	*Where's the bathroom/toilet?*	ˈdohn-deh ehs-ˈtah ehl ˈbah-nyoh
Por supuesto.	*Of course.*	pohr sooh-pooh-ˈehs-toh
No me gusta.	*I don't like it.*	noh meh ˈgoohs-tah
Nos gusta.	*We like it.*	nohs ˈgoohs-tah
¿A qué hora...?	*At what time...?*	ah keh ˈoh-rah
¿Cuándo...?	*When...?*	kooh-ˈahn-doh
¿Por qué?	*Why?*	pohr keh
Aquí	*Here*	ah-ˈkee

Listen to Track 3

¿Podría escribirlo por favor? (*formal*)	*Could you write it down, please?*	poh-ˈdree-ah ehs-kree-ˈbveer, pohr fah-ˈbvohr
¿Me lo escribe por favor? (*formal*)	*Will you please write it down for me?*	meh loh ehs-ˈkree-bveh pohr fah-ˈbvohr
De nada.	*You're welcome.*	deh ˈnah-dah

3

Esto es para tí. (*informal*) / Esto es para Usted. (*formal*)	*This is for you.*	'ehs-toh ehs 'pah-rah tee /'ehs-toh ehs 'pah-rah oohs-'tehd
Hay un error.	*There's a mistake.*	'a-ee oohn eh-'rrohr
Ahora	*Now*	ah-'oh-rah
Hoy/mañana/ la semana próxima	*Today/ tomorrow/next week*	'oh-ee/mah-'nyah-nah/lah seh-'mah-nah 'prohk-see-mah
¡Socorro! / ¡Pare! / ¡Váyase!	*Help! / Stop! / Go away!*	soh-'koh-rroh / 'pah-reh / 'bah-yah-seh
¿Dónde está...?	*Where is....?*	'dohn-deh ehs-'tah
Perfecto	*Perfect*	pehr-'fehk-toh
No necesito eso.	*I don't need that.*	noh neh-seh-'see-toh 'eh-soh
Es demasiado caro.	*It's too expensive.*	ehs deh-mah-see-'ah-doh 'kah-roh

Listen to Track 4

¿Cuántos años tienes (*informal*)? / tiene (*formal*)?	*How old are you?*	kooh-'ahn-tohs 'ah-nyohs tee-'eh-nehs / tee-'eh-neh
¿Cuánto cuesta esto?	*How much is this?*	kooh-'ahn-toh kooh-'eh-stah 'ehs-toh
¿Y ese?	*And that (one)?*	ee 'eh-seh

¿Podría repetirlo, por favor? *(formal)* / **¿Podrías** *(informal)* **repetirlo, por favor?**	*Could you repeat that, please?*	poh-'dree-ah rreh-peh-'teer-loh, pohr fah-'bvohr / poh-'dree-ahs rreh-peh-'teer-loh, pohr fah-'bvohr
¿Qué hora es?	*What time is it?*	keh 'oh-rah 'ehs
Son las __ de la tarde.	*It's _:oo PM.*	sohn lahs __ deh lah 'tahr-deh
Son las __ de la mañana.	*It's _:oo AM.*	sohn lahs __ deh lah mah-'nyah-nah
Son las __ y media.	*It's _:30.*	sohn lahs __ ee 'meh-dee-ah
Son las __ y cuarto.	*It's _:15.*	sohn lahs __ ee kooh-'ahr-toh
Es tarde.	*It's late.*	ehs 'tahr-deh
Es temprano.	*It's early.*	ehs tehm-'prah-noh
Más tarde	*Later*	mahs 'tahr-deh
¿Quién eres? / **¿Quién sos?** (vos) *(informal)*	*Who are you?*	kee-'en 'eh-rehs / kee-'ehn sohs
¿Quién es usted? *(formal)*	*Who are you?*	kee-'en ehs oohs-'tehd

CHAPTER 2: PROBLEMAS Y DIFICULTADES / PROBLEMS AND DIFFICULTIES

Listen to Track 5

Déjame en paz.	*Leave me alone.*	'deh-hah-meh ehn pahs
¡No me toques!	*Don't touch me!*	noh meh 'toh-kehs
Llamaré a la policía.	*I'll call the police.*	yah-mah-'reh ah lah poh-lee-'see-ah
¡Alto, ladrón!	*Stop! Thief!*	'ahl-toh, lah-'drohn
Necesito ayuda.	*I need help.*	neh-seh-'see-toh ah-'yooh-dah
Es una emergencia.	*It's an emergency.*	ehs 'ooh-nah eh-mehr-'hehn-see-ah
Estoy perdido/a.	*I'm lost.*	ehs-'toh-ee pehr-'dee-doh/ah
Perdí mi bolsa/bolso/cartera.	*I lost my purse/handbag.*	pehr-'dee mee 'bohl-sah/'bohl-soh/kahr-'teh-rah
Perdí mi cartera/billetera.	*I lost my wallet.*	pehr-'dee mee kahr-'teh-rah/bee-yeh-'teh-rah
Estoy enfermo/a.	*I'm sick.*	ehs-'toh-ee ehn-'fehr-moh/ah
Estoy herido/a.	*I've been injured.*	ehs-'toh-ee eh-'ree-doh/ah

Necesito un médico.	*I need a doctor.*	neh-seh-ˈsee-toh oohn ˈmeh-dee-koh
¿Puedo usar su teléfono? *(formal)* / ¿Puedo usar tu teléfono? *(informal)*	*Can I use your phone?*	pooh-ˈeh-doh ooh-ˈsahr sooh teh-ˈleh-foh-noh / pooh-ˈeh-doh ooh-ˈsahr tooh teh-ˈleh-foh-noh
¿Me presta su celular? *(formal)* / ¿Me prestas tu celular? *(informal)*	*Can I borrow your cell phone?*	meh ˈprehs-tah sooh seh-looh-ˈlahr / meh ˈprehs-tahs tooh seh-looh-ˈlahr

PART 2: SALUDOS, PRESENTACIÓN, CONVERSACIÓN SOCIAL / GREETINGS, INTRODUCTION, SOCIAL CONVERSATION

CHAPTER 3: ENCUENTROS Y SALUDOS / MEETING AND GREETING

Listen to Track 6

¡Buenos días!	_Good morning!_	booh-'eh-nohs 'dee-ahs
¡Buenas tardes!	_Good afternoon!_	booh-'eh-nahs 'tar-dehs
¡Buenas noches!	_Good evening! / Good night!_	booh-'eh-nahs 'noh-chehs
¡Hola!	_Hello!_	'oh-lah
Adiós.	_Goodbye._	ah-dee-'ohs
Hasta la vista. / Hasta luego.	_See you. / See you later._	'ahs-tah lah 'bees-tah / 'ahs-tah looh-'eh-goh
Hasta pronto.	_See you soon._	'ahs-tah 'prohn-toh
¡Nos vemos!	_See you!_	nohs 'beh-mohs
Hasta mañana.	_See you tomorrow._	'ahs-tah mah-'nyah-nah
¡Que te vaya bien! _(informal)_ / **¡Que le vaya bien!** _(formal)_	_Have a nice day!_	keh teh 'bah-yah bee-'ehn / keh leh 'bah-yah bee-'ehn
¡Que tengas un buen día! _(formal)_	_Have a nice day!_	keh 'tehn-gahs oohn booh-'ehn 'dee-ah

Fue un placer conocerte. (*informal*) / **Fue un placer conocerle.** (*formal*)	*It was a pleasure to meet you.*	fooh-ˈeh oohn plah-ˈsehr koh-noh-ˈsehr-the / fooh-ˈeh oohn plah-ˈsehr koh-noh-ˈsehr-leh
¡Cuánto tiempo!	*Long time no see!*	kooh-ˈahn-toh tee-ˈehm-poh
¡Cuídate!	*Take care!*	koohˈee-dah-teh

CHAPTER 4: CONOCIENDO A ALGUIEN / GETTING TO KNOW SOMEONE

<u>*Listen to Track 7*</u>

¿Cómo te llamas? *(informal)* / **¿Cómo se llama usted?** *(formal)*	*What is your name?*	'koh-moh teh 'yah-mahs /'koh-moh seh 'yah-mah oohs-'ted
¿Qué tal? *(informal)* / **¿Como estás?** *(informal)* / **¿Cómo está (usted)?** *(formal)*	*How are you?*	keh tahl /'koh-moh ehs-'tahs / 'koh-moh ehs-'tahs (oohs-'tehd)
Mi nombre es...	*My name is....*	mee 'nohm-breh ehs
¿De dónde eres? *(informal)* / **¿De dónde es (usted)?** *(formal)*	*Where are you from?*	deh 'dohn-deh 'eh-rehs / deh 'dohn-deh ehs (oohs-'tehd)
Soy de... Inglaterra/ los Estados Unidos/ Canadá.	*I'm from... England/the USA/Canada.*	'soh-ee deh... een-glah-'teh-rrah/lohs ehs-'tah-dohs ooh-'nee-dohs/ kah-nah-'dah

Somos de... Australia/ Irlanda.	We're from... Australia/ Ireland.	'soh-mohs deh... ah-oohs-'trah-lee-ah/eer-'lahn-dah
Estoy aquí de vacaciones.	I'm here on holidays.	ehs-'toh-ee ah-'kee deh bah-kah-see-'oh-nehs
¿Vives aquí? (informal) / ¿Vive aquí? (formal)	Do you live here?	'bee-bvehs ah-'kee / 'bee-bveh ah-'kee
¿Cuánto tiempo vas a estar aquí? (informal) / ¿Cuánto tiempo va a estar aquí? (formal)	How long are you going to stay here?	kooh-'ahn-toh tee-'ehm-poh bahs ah ehs-'tahr ah-'kee / kooh-'ahn-toh tee-'ehm-poh bah ah ehs-'tahr ah-'kee
Me voy a quedar una semana.	I'm going to stay here for one week.	meh 'boh-ee ah keh-'dahr 'ooh-nah seh-'mah-nah

Listen to Track 8

¿Te gusta el lugar? (informal) / ¿Le gusta el lugar? (formal)	Do you like it here?	teh 'goohs-tah ehl looh-'gahr / leh 'goohs-tah ehl looh-'gahr
¿Estás viajando solo/sola? (informal) / ¿Está viajando solo/sola? (formal)	Are you traveling by yourself?	ehs-'tahs bee-ah-'hahn-doh 'soh-loh/'soh-lah / ehs-'tah bee-ah-'hahn-doh 'soh-loh/'soh-lah

Estoy viajando con mi novio.	*I'm traveling with my boyfriend.*	ehs-'toh-ee bvee-ah-'hahn-doh 'kohn mee 'noh-bvee-oh
Estoy casada (f) / casado (m).	*I'm married.*	ehs-'toh-ee kah-'sah-dah / kah-'sah-doh
Estoy soltera (f) / soltero (m).	*I'm single.*	ehs-'toh-ee sohl-'teh-roh / sohl-'teh-rah
¿Vives con tu familia? (*informal*) / ¿Vive con su familia? (*formal*)	*Do you live with your family?*	'bee-bvehs kohn tooh fah-'mee-lee-ah / 'bee-bveh kohn sooh fah-'mee-lee-ah
¿Dónde te quedas? (*informal*) / ¿Dónde se queda? (*formal*)	*Where are you staying?*	'dohn-deh teh 'keh-dahs / 'dohn-deh seh 'keh-dah
Me quedo con unos amigos.	*I'm staying with some friends.*	meh 'keh-doh kohn 'ooh-nohs ah-'mee-gohs
Nos quedamos en un hotel en el centro.	*We're staying in a hotel in the center.*	nohs keh-'dah-mohs ehn oohn oh-'tehl ehn ehl 'sehn-troh

Listen to Track 9

¿Cuál es tu email? (*informal*) / ¿Cuál es su email? (*formal*)	*What is your email address?*	kooh-'ahl ehs tooh ee-'meh-ehl / kooh-'ahl ehs sooh ee-'meh-ehl

Este es mi número de celular.	*Here's my cell phone number.*	ˈehs-teh ehs mee ˈnooh-meh-roh deh seh-looh-ˈlahr
Mantengámo-nos en contacto.	*Let's keep in touch.*	mahn-tehn-ˈgah-moh-nohs ehn kohn-ˈtahk-toh
Te escribiré cuando llegue a... (*informal*) / Le escribiré cuando llegue a... (*formal*)	*I'll write you when I get to...*	teh ehs-kree-bee-ˈreh kooh-ˈahn-doh ˈyeh-geh ah / leh ehs-kree-bee-ˈreh kooh-ˈahn-doh ˈyeh-geh ah
¿A qué te dedicas? (*informal*) / ¿A qué se dedica? (*formal*)	*What do you do for a living?*	ah keh teh deh-ˈdee-kahs / ah keh seh deh-ˈdee-kah
Trabajo como (Traductor/ Hombre de Negocios).	*I work as a (translator/ businessman).*	trah-ˈbvah-hoh ˈkoh-moh (trah-doohk-ˈtohr/ ˈohm-breh deh neh-ˈgoh-see-ohs)
Me gusta el español.	*I like Spanish.*	meh ˈgoohs-tah ehl ehs-pah-ˈnyohl
Tengo un mes estudiando español.	*I've been learning Spanish for 1 month*	ˈtehn-goh oohn mehs ehs-tooh-dee-ˈahn-doh ehs-pah-ˈnyohl
!Oh, qué bueno!	*Oh! That's good!*	oh, keh booh-ˈeh-noh
Tengo (veinte, treinta...) años.	*I'm (twenty, thirty...) years old.*	ˈtehn-goh (ˈbeh-een-teh, ˈtreh-een-tah...) ˈah-nyohs

CHAPTER 5: BUENOS MODALES / GOOD MANNERS

<u>Listen to Track 10</u>

Por favor	*Please*	por fah-'bvohr
Muchas gracias.	*Thank you very much.*	'mooh-chahs 'grah-see-ahs
De nada. / No hay de que.	*You're welcome.*	deh 'nah-dah / noh 'a-ee deh keh
Con permiso.	*Excuse me.*	kohn pehr-'mee-soh
Salud.	*Bless you.*	sah-'loohd
Perdón	*Sorry*	pehr-'dohn
No necesitas preocuparte.	*No need to worry.*	noh neh-seh-'see-tas preh-ohk-ooh-'pahr-teh
Buenos días.	*Good morning.*	booh-'eh-nohs 'dee-ahs
Buenas tardes.	*Good afternoon.*	booh-'eh-nahs 'tahr-dehs
Buenas noches.	*Good night.*	booh-'eh-nahs 'noh-chehs

PART 3: CONOCIENDO A ALGUIEN / TRAVEL AND TRANSPORTATION

CHAPTER 6: EN EL AEROPUERTO / AT THE AIRPORT

Listen to Track 11

Busco la terminal uno.	*I'm looking for terminal one.*	ˈboohs-koh lah tehr-mee-ˈnahl ˈooh-noh
Esta terminal es para vuelos internacionales.	*This terminal is for international flights.*	ˈehs-tah tehr-mee-ˈnahl ehs ˈpah-rah booh-ˈeh-lohs een-tehr-nah-see-oh-ˈnah-lehs
Esta terminal es para vuelos locales/ nacionales.	*This terminal is for local flights.*	ˈehs-tah tehr-mee-ˈnahl ehs ˈpah-rah booh-ˈeh-lohs loh-ˈkah-lehs/nah-see-oh-ˈnah-lehs
¿Dónde están los carritos de equipaje?	*Where are the luggage carts located?*	ˈdohn-deh ehs-ˈtahn lohs kah-ˈrree-tohs deh eh-kee-ˈpah-heh
¿Cuándo sale el próximo vuelo para México?	*When is the next flight to Mexico?*	kooh-ˈahn-doh ˈsah-leh ehl ˈprohk-see-moh booh-ˈeh-loh ˈpah-rah ˈmeh-hee-koh
¿Es un vuelo directo?	*Is it a direct flight?*	ehs oohn booh-ˈeh-loh dee-ˈrehk-toh

17

¿Cuánto tiempo habrá de retraso?	How long will it be delayed?	kooh-'ahn-toh tee-'ehm-poh ah-'brah deh reh-'trah-soh
¿Por qué se tarda tanto?	Why is it taking so long?	pohr keh seh 'tahr-dah 'tahn-toh
Prefiero un asiento de pasillo.	I prefer an aisle seat.	preh-fee-'eh-roh oohn ah-see-'ehn-toh deh pah-'see-oh
Prefiero un asiento de ventana.	I prefer a window seat.	Preh-fee-'eh-roh oohn ah-see-'ehn-toh deh behn-'tah-nah

Listen to Track 12

Tengo dos maletas. / Llevo dos maletas.	I have two bags with me.	'tehn-goh dohs mah-'leh-tahs / 'yeh-bvoh dohs mah-'leh-tahs
Es mi maletín. / Es mi equipaje de mano.	That's my carry-on bag.	ehs mee mah-leh-'teen / ehs mee eh-kee-'pah-heh deh 'mah-noh
¿Puedo llevar esto como equipaje de mano?	Can I take this as carry-on luggage?	pooh-'eh-doh yeh-'bvahr 'ehs-toh 'koh-moh eh-kee-'pah-heh deh 'mah-noh
Perdí mi pase de abordar.	I lost my boarding pass.	pehr-'dee mee 'pah-seh deh ah-bohr-'dahr

¿Cuánto dura el vuelo a Caracas?	How long is the flight to Caracas?	kooh-'ahn-toh 'dooh-rah ehl booh-'eh-loh ah ka-'rah-kahs
Ese es mi asiento.	That's my seat.	'eh-seh ehs mee ah-see-'ehn-toh
¿Dónde puedo reclamar mi equipaje?	Where can I claim my luggage?	'dohn-deh pooh-'eh-doh rreh-klah-'mahr mee eh-kee-'pah-heh
¿En qué banda puedo recoger mi equipaje?	From which conveyor belt can I pick up my luggage?	ehn keh 'bahn-dah pooh-'eh-doh rreh-koh-'hehr mee eh-kee-'pah-heh
Mis maletas no han llegado.	My luggage hasn't arrived.	mees mah-'leh-tahs noh ahn yeh-'gah-doh

Listen to Track 13

Se perdieron mis maletas.	My luggage has been lost.	seh pehr-dee-'eh-rohn mees mah-'leh-tahs
¿Dónde está la aduana?	Where is customs?	'dohn-deh ehs-'tah lah ah-dooh-'ah-nah
Estoy viajando solo.	I'm traveling on my own.	ehs-'toh-ee bee-ah-'hahn-doh 'soh-loh
Estoy viajando con mi esposa/ esposo.	I'm traveling with my wife/ husband.	ehs-'toh-ee bee-ah-'hahn-doh kohn mee ehs-'poh-sah/ehs-'poh-soh

Estoy aquí de negocios.	*I'm here on business.*	ehs-'toh-ee ah-'kee deh neh-'goh-see-ohs
Estoy aquí de vacaciones.	*I'm here on holiday.*	ehs-'toh-ee ah-'kee deh bah-kah-see-'oh-nehs
Voy a estar dos semanas. / Estoy aquí por dos semanas.	*I'm here for two weeks.*	'boh-ee ah ehs-'tahr dohs seh-'mah-nahs / ehs-'toh-ee ah-'kee pohr dohs seh-'mah-nahs
Voy a estar tres días. / Estoy aquí por tres días.	*I'm here for three days.*	boh-'ee ah ehs-'tahr trehs 'dee-ahs / ehs-'toh-ee ah-'kee pohr trehs 'dee-ahs
No tengo nada qué declarar.	*I have nothing to declare.*	noh 'tehn-goh 'nah-dah keh deh-klah-'rahr

CHAPTER 7: TOMANDO EL AUTOBUS / TAKING THE BUS

Listen to Track 14

Dos boletos para Lima, por favor.	*Two tickets to Lima, please.*	dohs boh-'leh-tohs 'pah-rah 'lee-mah, pohr fah-'bvohr
¿De dónde sale el autobús para Bogotá?	*Where does the bus to Bogotá leave from?*	deh 'dohn-deh 'sah-leh ehl a-ooh-toh-'bvoohs 'pah-rah boh-goh-'tah
¿A qué hora sale el próximo autobús?	*What time does the next bus leave?*	ah keh 'oh-rah 'sah-leh ehl 'prohk-see-moh a-ooh-toh-'bvoohs
¿A qué hora sale el último autobús?	*What time does the last bus leave?*	ah keh 'oh-rah 'sah-leh ehl 'oohl-tee-moh a-ooh-toh-'bvoohs
¿Cuál autobús va a Tegucigalpa?	*Which bus goes to Tegucigalpa?*	kooh-'ahl a-ooh-toh-'bvoohs bah ah teh-gooh-see-'gahl-pah
¿No hay boletos más baratos?	*You don't have any cheaper tickets?*	noh 'a-ee boh-'leh-tohs mahs bah-'rah-tohs
¿Este asiento reclina?	*Does this seat recline?*	'ehs-teh ah-see-'ehn-toh rreh-'klee-nah

¿Cuánto dura el viaje?	How long is the trip?	kooh-'ahn-toh dooh-rah ehl bee-'a-heh
¿Es un viaje directo?	Is it a direct route?	ehs oohn bee-'a-heh dee-'rehk-toh
¿Tengo que cambiar de autobús?	Do I have to change buses?	'tehn-goh keh kahm-bee-'ahr deh a-ooh-toh-'bvoohs
¿Para el autobús en Guanajuato?	Does this bus stop in Guanajuato?	'pah-rah ehl a-ooh-toh-'bvoohs ehn gooh-a-nah-hooh-'ah-toh
¿A qué hora llega a...?	What time does it get to...?	ah keh 'oh-rah 'yeh-gah ah

Listen to Track 15

¿Dónde puedo comprar un boleto?	Where can I buy a ticket?	'dohn-deh pooh-'eh-doh kohm-'prahr oohn boh-'leh-toh
¿Dónde está la taquilla?	Where's the ticket window/office?	'dohn-deh ehs-'tah lah tah-'kee-yah
¿Cuál autobús va al centro?	Which bus goes to the center?	kooh-'ahl a-ooh-toh-'bvoohs bah ahl 'sehn-troh
¿Dónde está la parada?	Where is the bus stop?	'dohn-deh ehs-'tah lah pah-'rah-dah
¿Va al centro?	Do you go to the downtown?	bah ahl 'sehn-troh

¿Cuántas paradas son al centro?	*How many stops to the downtown?*	kooh-'ahn-tahs pah-'rah-dahs sohn ahl 'sehn-troh
¿Dónde se venden fichas?	*Where do I buy tokens?*	'dohn-deh seh 'behn-dehn 'fee-chahs
¿Cuánto cuesta el pasaje?	*What's the fare?*	kooh-'ahn-toh kooh-'ehs-tah ehl pah-'sah-heh
¿Me puede avisar cuando lleguemos al centro?	*Can you tell me when we get to the center?*	meh pooh-'eh-deh ah-bvee-'sahr kooh-'ahn-doh yeh-'geh-mohs ahl 'sehn-troh
¿Dónde está la estación de metro?	*Where's the metro station?*	'dohn-deh ehs-'tah lah ehs-tah-see-'ohn deh 'meh-troh
¡Espere!	*Hold on! / Wait!*	ehs-'peh-reh
Aquí me bajo, por favor.	*I want to get off here, please.*	ah-'kee meh 'bah-hoh, pohr fah-'bvohr

CHAPTER 8: TOMANDO UN TAXI / TAKING A TAXI

Listen to Track 16

Quisiera un taxi a las ocho de la noche.	*I would like a taxi at 8 p.m.*	kee-see-'eh-rah oohn 'tahk-see ah lahs 'oh-choh deh lah 'noh-chehs
Quisiera un taxi tan pronto como sea posible.	*I would like a taxi as soon as possible.*	kee-see-'eh-rah oohn 'tahk-see tahn 'prohn-toh 'koh-moh 'seh-ah poh-'see-bleh
¿Está libre este taxi?	*Is this taxi free?*	ehs-'tah 'lee-breh 'ehs-teh 'tahk-see
La esquina de Hidalgo y Bolívar.	*The corner of Hidalgo and Bolívar.*	lah ehs-'kee-nah deh ee-'dahl-goh ee boh-'lee-bvahr
¿Cuánto cuesta ir al centro?	*How much is it to the center?*	kooh-'ahn-toh kooh-'ehs-tah eer ahl 'sehn-troh
¿Tiene un taxímetro? / Usa el taxímetro?	*Do you have a meter? / Do you use your meter?*	tee-'eh-neh oohn tahk-'see-meh-troh /'ooh-sah ehl tahk-'see-meh-troh
Espere aquí, por favor.	*Wait here, please.*	ehs-'peh-reh ah-'kee, pohr fah-'bvohr
Pare en el próximo semáforo, por favor.	*Stop at the next traffic light, please.*	'pah-reh ehn ehl 'prohk-see-moh seh-'mah-foh-roh, pohr fah-'bvohr

Pare aquí, por favor.	*Stop here, please.*	ˈpah-reh ah-ˈkee, pohr fah-ˈbvohr
El taxímetro marca veinte (20) pesos.	*The meter shows 20 pesos.*	ehl tahk-ˈsee-meh-troh ˈmahr-kah ˈbeh-een-teh ˈpeh-sohs
¡Estafador!	*Swindler!*	ehs-tah-fah-ˈdohr

CHAPTER 9: ALQUILANDO UN AUTO / RENTING A CAR

Listen to Track 17

¿Dónde se puede rentar un coche?	*Where can I rent a car?*	'dohn-deh seh pooh-'eh-deh rrenh-'tahr oohn 'koh-cheh
Quisiera rentar una moto.	*I'd like to rent a motorbike.*	kee-see-'eh-rah rrehn-'tahr 'ooh-nah 'moh-toh
Quisiera rentar un coche automático.	*I'd like to rent an automatic car.*	kee-see-'eh-rah rrehn-'tahr oohn 'koh-cheh a-ooh-toh-'mah-tee-koh
Quisiera rentar un coche manual.	*I'd like to rent a manual car.*	kee-see-'eh-rah rrehn-'tahr oohn 'koh-cheh mah-nooh-'ahl
¿Qué modelo es?	*What model is it?*	keh moh-'deh-loh ehs
¿Tiene un coche con aire acondicionado?	*Do you have a car with air conditioning?*	tee-'eh-neh oohn 'koh-cheh kohn 'a-ee-reh ah-kohn-dee-see-oh-'nah-doh
¿Cuánto cuesta la renta por un día?	*How much does it cost to rent for one day?*	kooh-'ahn-toh kooh-'ehs-tah lah 'rrehn-tah pohr oohn 'dee-ah

¿Cuánto cuesta la renta por una semana?	*How much does it cost to rent for a week?*	kooh-'ahn-toh kooh-'ehs-tah lah 'rrehn-tah pohr 'ooh-nah seh-'mah-nah
¿Se incluye seguro en el precio?	*Is insurance included in the price?*	seh een-'klooh-yeh seh-'gooh-roh ehn ehl 'preh-see-oh
¿El tanque está lleno?	*Is the tank full?*	ehl 'tahn-keh ehs-'tah 'yeh-noh

CHAPTER 10: EN AUTO / CAR DRIVING

Listen to Track *18*

¿Por aquí se va a Montevideo?	*Is this the road to Montevideo?*	pohr ah-'kee seh bah ah mohn-teh-'bvee-deh-oh
¿Cómo se llega a la carretera a Guadalajara?	*How do I get to the highway to Guadalajara?*	'koh-moh seh 'yeh-gah ah lah kah-rreh-'teh-rah ah gooh-ah-dah-lah-'hah-rah
¿Dónde hay una gasolinera por aquí?	*Where is there a gas station around here?*	dohn-deh 'a-ee 'ooh-nah gah-soh-lee-'neh-rah pohr ah-'kee
Me quedé sin gasolina.	*I've run out of gas.*	meh keh-'deh seen gah-soh-'lee-nah
Lleno, por favor.	*Fill it up, please.*	'yeh-noh, pohr fah-'bvohr
Quiero 50 pesos.	*I'd like 50 pesos worth.*	kee-'eh-roh seen-kooh-'ehn-tah 'peh-sohs
Gasolina sin plomo, por favor.	*Unleaded gas/ petrol, please.*	gah-soh-'lee-nah seen 'ploh-moh, pohr fah-'bvohr
Diésel	*Diesel*	dee-'eh-sehl
Revise el nivel de aceite, por favor.	*Check the oil, please.*	rreh-'bvee-seh ehl nee-'bvel deh ahh-'seh-ee-teh, pohr fah-'bvohr

¿Dónde puedo revisar la presión de las llantas?	Where can I check my tire pressure?	'dohn-deh pooh-'eh-doh rreh-bvee-'sahr lah preh-see-'ohn deh lahs 'yahn-tahs
¿Dónde se paga?	Where do I pay?	'dohn-deh seh 'pah-gah

Listen to Track 19

Mi coche no arranca.	My car doesn't start.	mee 'koh-cheh noh ah-'rrahn-kah
Nuestro coche se descompuso.	Our car broke down.	nooh-'ehs-troh 'koh-cheh seh dehs-kohm-'pooh-soh
Dejé las llaves dentro del coche.	I've locked the keys inside.	deh-'heh lahs 'yah-bvehs 'dehn-troh dehl 'koh-cheh
La batería se agotó.	The battery died.	lah bah-teh-'ree-ah seh ah-goh-'toh
Tengo una llanta ponchada. / Se me ponchó una llanta.	I have a flat tire.	'tehn-goh 'ooh-nah 'yahn-tah pohn-'chah-dah / seh meh pohn-'choh 'ooh-nah 'yahn-tah
Mis limpia-parabrisas/ limpiadores no sirven.	My (windshield) wipers won't work.	mees leem-pee-ah-pah-rah-'bree-sahs/leem-pee-ah-'doh-rehs noh 'seer-bvehn

¿Cuánto tiempo puedo estacionarme aquí?	*How long can I park here?*	kooh-'ahn-toh tee-'ehm-poh pooh-'eh-doh ehs-tah-see-oh-'nahr-meh ah-'kee
¿Hay un mecánico cerca de aquí?	*Is there a garage/mechanic nearby?*	'a-ee oohn meh-'kah-nee-koh 'sehr-kah deh ah-'kee
¿Puede arreglarlo?	*Can you fix it?*	pooh-'eh-deh ah-rreh-'glahr-loh
¿Cuánto tardará?	*How long will it take?*	kooh-'ahn-toh tahr-dah-'rah
¿Cuánto cuesta esa refacción?	*How much does this part cost?*	kooh-'ahn-toh kooh-'ehs-tah 'eh-sah rreh-fahk-see-'ohn

CHAPTER 11: PREGUNTANDO POR DIRECCIONES / ASKING FOR DIRECTIONS

Listen to Track 20

¿Conoces esta región?	*Do you know this area?*	koh-'noh-sehs 'ehs-tah rreh-hee-'ohn
¿Hay un supermercado por aquí?	*Is there a supermarket nearby?*	'a-ee oohn sooh-pehr-mehr-'kah-doh pohr ah-'kee
¿Hay un banco por aquí?	*Is there a bank around here?*	'a-ee oohn 'bahn-koh pohr ah-'kee
¿Está lejos de aquí?	*Is it far from here?*	ehs-'tah 'leh-hohs deh ah-'kee
¿Cómo llego a la catedral?	*How do I get to the cathedral?*	'koh-moh 'yeh-goh ah lah kah-teh-'drahl
Busco esta calle.	*I'm looking for this street.*	'boohs-koh 'ehs-tah 'kah-yeh
¿A qué distancia está?	*How far is it?*	ah keh dees-'tahn-see-ah ehs-'tah
Está a dos cuadras.	*It's two blocks from here.*	ehs-'tah ah dohs kooh-'ah-drahs
Está todo derecho.	*It's straight ahead.*	ehs-'tah 'toh-doh deh-'reh-choh
De vuelta a la izquierda en la próxima calle.	*Turn left at the next street.*	deh booh-'ehl-tah ah lah ees-kee-'ehr-dah ehn lah 'prohk-see-mah 'kah-yeh

De vuelta a la derecha en el semáforo.	*Turn right at the traffic lights.*	deh booh-'ehl-tah ah lah deh-'reh-chah ehn ehl seh-'mah-foh-roh
El restaurante está en la esquina.	*The restaurant is on the corner.*	ehl rrehs-ta-ooh-'rahn-teh ehs-'tah ehn lah ehs-'kee-nah
El hotel está al lado del banco.	*The hotel is next to the bank.*	ehl oh-'tehl ehs-'tah ahl 'lah-doh dehl 'bahn-koh

Listen to Track 21

La tienda está en frente de su hotel.	*The store is in front of your hotel.*	lah tee-'ehn-dah ehs-'tah ehn 'frehn-teh deh sooh oh-'tehl
Está muy cerca.	*It's very close.*	ehs-'tah 'mooh-ee 'sehr-kah
Está lejos.	*It's far.*	ehs-'tah 'leh-hohs
Demasiado lejos para caminar.	*Too far to walk.*	deh-mah-see-'ah-doh 'leh-hohs 'pah-rah kah-mee-'nahr
El museo está detrás de la oficina de correos.	*The museum is behind the post office.*	ehl mooh-'seh-oh ehs-'tah deh-'trahs deh lah oh-fee-'see-nah deh koh-'rreh-ohs
Vaya por acá.	*Go this way.*	'bah-yah pohr ah-'kah

El zoológico está a una hora en coche.	The zoo is one hour by car.	ehl soh-oh-ˈloh-hee-koh ehs-ˈtah ah ˈooh-nah ˈoh-rah ehn ˈkoh-cheh
¿Puedo ir al centro a pie desde aquí?	Can I walk to the downtown from here?	pooh-ˈeh-doh eer ahl ˈsehn-troh ah pee-ˈeh ˈdehs-deh ah-ˈkee
El centro está a veinte minutos a pie.	Downtown is a twenty minutes walk from here.	ehl ˈsehn-troh ehs-ˈtah ah ˈbeh-een-teh mee-ˈnooh-tohs ah pee-ˈeh
La estación de metro está por ahí.	The metro station is that way.	lah ehs-tah-see-ˈohn deh ˈmeh-troh ehs-ˈtah pohr a-ˈee
Baje en la tercera estación.	Get off at the third station.	ˈbah-heh ehn lah tehr-ˈseh-rah ehs-tah-see-ˈohn
Siga derecho hasta la intersección.	Keep going straight until the intersection.	ˈsee-gah deh-ˈreh-choh ˈahs-tah lah een-tehr-sek-see-ˈohn

PART 4: OCIO, CULTURA Y ENTRETENIMIENTO / LEISURE, CULTURE AND ENTERTAINMENT

CHAPTER 12: SENDERISMO AL AIRE LIBRE / OUTDOOR HIKING

Listen to Track 22

¿Dónde puedo obtener un mapa de esta zona/región?	_Where can I get a map of this region?_	ˈdohn-deh pooh-ˈeh-doh ohbv-teh-ˈnehr oohn ˈmah-pah deh ˈehs-tah ˈsoh-nah/rreh-hee-ˈohn
¿Hay rutas para excursionismo por aquí?	_Are there any hiking trails around here?_	ˈa-ee ˈrrooh-tahs ˈpah-rah ehk-skoohr-see-oh-ˈnees-moh pohr ah-ˈkee
¿Hay rutas para ciclismo de montaña?	_Are there any trails for mountain biking?_	ˈa-ee ˈrrooh-tahs ˈpah-rah see-ˈklees-moh deh mohn-ˈtah-nyah
¿Cuál ruta es la más difícil?	_Which route is the most difficult?_	kooh-ˈahl ˈrrooh-tah ehs lah mahs dee-ˈfee-seel
¿Está bien marcada esta ruta?	_Is this track well marked?_	ehs-ˈtah bee-ˈehn mahr-ˈkah-dah ˈehs-tah ˈrrooh-tah
¿Puedo atravesar por aquí?	_Can I go through here?_	pooh-ˈeh-doh ah-trah-bveh-ˈsahr pohr ah-ˈkee
¿Es muy empinada la subida?	_Is the climb very steep?_	ehs ˈmooh-ee ehm-pee-ˈnah-dah lah sooh-ˈbvee-dah

¿Qué tan larga es la ruta?	*How long is the trail?*	keh tahn 'lahr-gah ehs lah 'rrooh-tah
¿Hay una cabaña donde podemos quedarnos?	*Is there a cabin where we can stay overnight?*	'a-ee 'ooh-nah kah-'bvah-nyah 'dohn-deh poh-'deh-mohs keh-'dahr-nohs
Estamos perdidos.	*We're lost.*	ehs-'tah-mohs pehr-'dee-dohs

CHAPTER 13: VISITANDO LUGARES DE INTERÉS / SIGHTSEEING

Listen to Track 23

Quisiera comprar un mapa de la zona.	_I would like to buy a local map._	kee-see-ˈeh-rah kohm-ˈprahr oohn ˈmah-pah deh lah ˈsoh-nah
Me gustaría ver el museo.	_I'd like to see the museum._	meh goohs-tah-ˈree-ah behr ehl mooh-ˈseh-oh
¿Qué es eso?	_What is that?_	keh ehs ˈeh-soh
¿Qué es este edificio?	_What is this building?_	keh ehs ˈehs-teh eh-dee-ˈfee-see-oh
¿A qué hora abren?	_What time does it open?_	ah keh ˈoh-rah ˈah-brehn
¿Cuánto cuesta la entrada?	_How much do you charge for admission?_	kooh-ˈahn-toh kooh-ˈehs-tah lah ehn-ˈtrah-dah
¿A qué hora cierran?	_What time do you close?_	ah keh ˈoh-rah see-ˈeh-rrahn
¿Hay descuento para estudiantes?	_Is there a discount for students?_	ˈa-ee dehs-kooh-ˈehn-toh ˈpah-rah ehs-tooh-dee-ˈahn-tehs
¿Puedo tomar fotos aquí?	_Can I take photographs here?_	pooh-ˈeh-doh toh-ˈmahr ˈfoh-tohs ah-ˈkee
¿Puedo contratar un guía?	_Can I hire a guide?_	pooh-ˈeh-doh kohn-trah-ˈtahr oohn ˈgee-ah

¿Tiene folletos con información sobre el museo?	*Do you have brochures with information about the museum?*	tee-'eh-neh foh-'yeh-tohs kohn een-fohr-mah-see-'ohn 'soh-breh ehl mooh-'seh-oh

CHAPTER 14: PLAYA / BEACH

Listen to Track 24

¿Dónde está la mejor playa para surfear?	*Where is the best surfing beach?*	'dohn-deh ehs-'tah lah meh-'hohr 'plah-yah 'pah-rah soohr-feh-'ahr
¿Dónde está la playa más cercana?	*Where is the nearest beach?*	'dohn-deh ehs-'tah lah 'plah-yah mahs sehr-'kah-nah
¿Dónde está el mejor lugar para bucear?	*Where is the best place for scuba diving?*	'dohn-deh ehs-'tah ehl meh-'hohr looh-'gahr 'pah-rah booh-seh-'ahr
¿Es seguro nadar aquí?	*Is it safe to swim here?*	ehs seh-'gooh-roh nah-'dahr ah-'kee
No es seguro. No te lo recomiendo.	*It's not safe. I don't recommend it.*	noh ehs seh-'gooh-roh. Noh teh loh reh-koh-mee-'ehn-doh
Es muy peligroso echarse clavados aquí.	*It's very dangerous to dive here.*	ehs 'mooh-ee peh-lee-'groh-soh eh-'chahr-seh klah-'bvah-dohs ah-'kee
¿Es limpia esta agua?	*Is the water clean here?*	ehs 'leem-pee-ah 'ehs-tah 'ah-gooh-ah

¿Hay sanitarios en la playa?	*Are there toilets on the beach?*	'a-ee sah-nee-'tah-ree-ohs ehn lah 'plah-yah
¿Cuánto cuesta rentar una silla?	*How much does it cost to rent a beach chair?*	kooh-'ahn-toh kooh-'ehs-tah rrehn-'tahr 'ooh-nah 'see-yah
¿Es venenosa/ peligrosa esta medusa/ aguamala?	*Is this jellyfish poisonous/ dangerous?*	ehs beh-neh-'noh-sah/peh-lee-'groh-sah 'ehs-tah meh-'dooh-sah/ah-gooh-ah-'mah-lah
¿Hay algún salvavidas en esta playa?	*Is there a lifeguard on this beach?*	'a-ee ahl-'goohn sahl-bvah-'bvee-dahs ehn 'ehs-tah 'plah-yah

PART 5: UN LUGAR PARA ALOJARSE / A PLACE TO STAY

CHAPTER 15: BUSCANDO UN HOTEL / LOOKING FOR A HOTEL

Listen to Track 25

¿Me puede recomendar un hotel bueno y barato por aquí?	*Can you recommend a good, cheap hotel around here?*	meh pooh-'eh-deh rreh-koh-mehn-'dahr oohn oh-'tehl booh-'eh-noh ee bah-'rah-toh pohr ah-'kee
¿Hay un hostal cerca de aquí?	*Is there a hostel nearby?*	'a-ee oohn ohs-'tahl 'sehr-kah deh ah-'kee
Quisiera reservar una habitación por 4 noches, por favor.	*I'd like to book a room for 4 nights, please.*	kee-see-'eh-rah rreh-sehr-'bvahr ooh-nah ah-bvee-tah-see-'ohn pohr kooh-'ah-troh 'noh-chehs, pohr fah-'bvohr
¿Tiene una habitación sencilla?	*Do you have a single room?*	tee-'eh-neh 'ooh-nah ah-bvee-tah-see-'ohn sehn-'see-yah
¿Cuánto cuesta una habitación doble/para 2 personas por noche?	*How much is a double room/a room for 2 people per night?*	kooh-'ahn-toh kooh-'ehs-tah 'ooh-nah ah-bvee-tah-see-'ohn 'doh-bleh/ 'pah-rah dohs pehr-'soh-nahs pohr 'noh-cheh

42

¿Pueden dormir tres personas en esta habitación?	*Can three people stay in this room?*	pooh-ˈeh-dehn dohr-ˈmeer trehs pehr-ˈsoh-nahs ehn ˈehs-tah ah-bvee-tah-see-ˈohn
¿Cuánto cuesta una habitación doble con camas individuales?	*How much is a double room with separate beds?*	kooh-ˈahn-toh kooh-ˈehs-tah ˈooh-nah ah-bvee-tah-see-ˈohn ˈdoh-bleh kohn ˈkah-mahs een-dee-bvee-dooh-ˈah-lehs
¿Tiene una habitación con baño?	*Do you have a room with a bathroom?*	tee-ˈeh-neh ˈooh-nah ah-bvee-tah-see-ˈohn kohn ˈbah-nyoh
¿Cuánto es el cargo diario?	*What is the charge per day?*	kooh-ˈahn-toh ehs ehl ˈkahr-goh dee-ˈah-ree-oh
¿Hay una habitación con aire acondicionado?	*Do you have a room with air conditioning?*	ˈa-ee ˈooh-nah ah-bvee-tah-see-ˈohn kohn ˈa-ee-reh ah-kohn-dee-see-oh-ˈnah-doh

Listen to Track 26

¿Podría ver la habitación? / ¿Puedo verla?	*Could I see the room? / Can I see it?*	poh-ˈdree-ah behr lah ah-bvee-tah-see-ˈohn / pooh-ˈeh-doh ˈbehr-lah
Está bien, la tomo.	*It's fine, I'll take it.*	ehs-ˈtah bee-ˈehn, lah ˈtoh-moh

¿Aceptan tarjetas de crédito?	*Do you accept credit cards?*	ah-'sehp-tahn tahr-'heh-tahs deh 'kreh-dee-toh
¿Necesito pagar por adelantado?	*Do I have to pay upfront?*	neh-seh-'see-toh pah-'gahr pohr ah-deh-lahn-'tah-doh
¿A qué hora hay que dejar la habitación?	*What time is checkout?*	ah keh 'oh-rah 'a-ee keh deh-'hahr lah ah-bvee-tah-see-'ohn
¿Cuándo se sirve el desayuno?	*When is breakfast served?*	kooh-'ahn-doh seh 'seer-beh ehl deh-sah-'yooh-noh
Por favor, despiérteme a las seis de la mañana.	*Please wake me up at 6:00 AM.*	pohr fah-'bvohr, dehs-pee-'ehr-teh-meh ah lahs 'seh-ees deh lah mah-'nyah-nah
¿Hay una lavandería aquí?	*Is there a laundry room here?*	'a-ee 'ooh-nah lah-bvanh-deh-'ree-ah ah-'kee
¿Puedo usar la piscina?	*Can I use the swimming pool?*	pooh-'eh-doh ooh-'sahr lah pee-'see-nah

CHAPTER 16: PROBLEMAS EN EL HOTEL / PROBLEMS AT THE HOTEL

Listen to Track 27

Perdí la llave.	_I lost the key._	pehr-'dee lah 'yah-bveh
El ventilador no funciona.	_The fan doesn't work._	ehl behn-tee-lah-'dohr noh foohn-see-'oh-nah
No hay toallas en mi habitación.	_There are no towels in my room._	noh 'a-ee toh-'ah-yahs ehn mee ah-bvee-tah-see-'ohn
Estas toallas no están limpias.	_These towels are not clean._	'ehs-tahs toh-'ah-yahs noh ehs-'tahn 'leem-pee-ahs
¿Podría darme otra cobija/ manta?	_Could you give me another blanket?_	poh-'dree-ah 'dahr-meh 'oh-trah koh-'bvee-hah/'mahn-tah
Hay mucho ruido.	_It's very noisy._	'a-ee 'mooh-choh rrooh-'ee-doh
La habitación es muy oscura.	_The room is very dark._	lah ah-bvee-tah-see-'ohn ehs 'mooh-ee ohs-kooh-rah
La televisión no funciona/no sirve.	_The TV doesn't work._	lah teh-leh-bvee-see-'ohn noh foohn-see-'oh-nah/noh 'seer-beh

No hay agua caliente en el baño.	*There's no hot water in the bathroom.*	noh 'a-ee 'ah-gooh-ah kah-lee-'ehn-teh ehn ehl 'bah-nyoh
Esa habitación huele muy mal.	*That room smells very bad.*	'eh-sah ah-bvee-tah-see-'ohn ooh-'eh-leh 'mooh-ee mahl
¿Me permite cambiar de habitación?	*Can I change rooms?*	meh pehr-'mee-teh kahm-bee-'ahr deh ah-bvee-tah-see-'ohn

CHAPTER 17: CHECK OUT DEL HOTEL / HOTEL CHECK OUT

Listen to Track 28

¿Podría dejar la habitación más tarde?	*Could I check out later?*	poh-'dree-ah deh-'hahr lah ah-bvee-tah-see-'ohn mahs 'tahr-deh
¿Puedo dejar mi equipaje hasta las dos?	*Can I leave my luggage until 2?*	pooh-'eh-doh deh-'hahr mee eh-kee-'pah-heh 'ahs-tah lahs dohs
¿Nos puede devolver nuestros pasaportes, por favor?	*May we have our passports back, please?*	nohs pooh-'eh-deh deh-bvohl-'behr nooh-'ehs-trohs pah-sah-'pohr-tehs, pohr fah-'bvohr
¿Me da un recibo, por favor?	*Can I get a receipt, please?*	meh dah oohn reh-'see-bvoh, pohr fah-'bvohr
¿Me podría pedir un taxi al aeropuerto?	*Could you call me a taxi to the airport?*	meh poh-'dree-ah peh-'deer oohn 'tahk-see ahl ah-eh-roh-pooh-'ehr-toh
Para las ocho de la mañana.	*For 8:00 AM.*	'pah-rah lahs 'oh-choh deh lah mah-'nyah-nah
Ahorita.	*Right now.*	ah-oh-'ree-tah

Ha sido muy amable.	*You've been very nice.*	ah 'see-doh 'mooh-ee ah-'mah-bleh
¡Muchas gracias! Tuvimos una estancia muy agradable.	*Thank you very much! We had a very pleasant stay.*	'mooh-chahs 'grah-see-ahs! tooh-'bvee-mohs 'ooh-nah ehs-'tahn-see-ah 'mooh-ee ah-grah-'dah-bleh

CHAPTER 18: ALOJAMIENTOS BARATOS (CAMPAMENTOS, HOSTALES, ETC.) / CHEAP ACCOMMODATIONS (CAMPING, HOSTELS, ETC.)

Listen to Track 29

¿Hay un albergue juvenil/un hostal por aquí?	*Is there a youth hostel around here?*	ˈa-ee oohn ahl-ˈbvehr-geh hooh-bveh-ˈneel/oohn ohs-ˈtahl pohr ah-ˈkee
¿Puede recomendarme un lugar barato para quedarme?	*Can you recommend a cheap place to stay?*	pooh-ˈeh-deh rreh-koh-mehn-ˈdahr-meh oohn looh-ˈgahr bah-ˈrah-toh ˈpah-rah keh-ˈdahr-meh
¿Me puedo quedar una noche en su casa?	*Can I stay one night at your place?*	meh pooh-ˈeh-doh keh-ˈdahr ˈooh-nah ˈnoh-cheh ehn sooh ˈkah-sah
Tengo mi propia bolsa de dormir.	*I have my own sleeping bag.*	ˈtehn-goh mee ˈproh-pee-ah ˈbohl-sah deh dohr-ˈmeer
¿Hay un área para acampar cerca de aquí?	*Is there a campground nearby?*	ˈa-ee oohn ˈah-reh-ah ˈpah-rah ah-kahm-ˈpahr ˈsehr-kah deh ah-ˈkee

Un lugar de acampado.	A camp site.	oohn looh-ˈgahr deh ah-kahm-ˈpah-doh
¿Se puede acampar aquí?	Can I camp here?	seh pooh-ˈeh-deh ah-kahm-ˈpahr ah-ˈkee
¿Cuánto es por tienda?	How much is it for a tent?	kooh-ˈahn-toh ehs pohr tee-ˈehn-dah
¿Podría estacionar al lado de la tienda?	Could I park next to my tent?	poh-ˈdree-ah ehs-tah-see-oh-ˈnahr ahl ˈlah-doh deh lah tee-ˈehn-dah
¿Tiene electricidad?	Do you have electricity?	tee-ˈeh-neh eh-lehk-tree-see-ˈdahd
¿Dónde están los sanitarios?	Where are the restrooms/ toilets?	ˈdohn-deh ehs-ˈtahn lohs sah-nee-ˈtah-ree-ohs

PART 6: HABLAR ACERCA DE LA HORA DE LA COMIDA Y DE COMER / TALKING ABOUT MEALTIMES AND EATING

CHAPTER 19: TÉRMINOS GENERALES / GENERAL TERMS

Listen to Track 30

Tengo mucha hambre.	_I'm very hungry._	'tehn-goh 'mooh-chah 'ahm-breh
Tengo sed.	_I'm thirsty._	'tehn-goh sehd
Tengo ganas de tomar un café. / Se me antoja un café.	_I feel like drinking coffee._	'tehn-goh 'gah-nahs deh toh-'mahr oohn kah-'feh / seh meh ahn-'toh-hah oohn kah-'feh
Estoy satisfecho/ bien.	_I'm full._	ehs-'toh-ee sah-tees-'feh-choh/ bee-'ehn
No tenemos hambre.	_We're not hungry._	noh tehn-'ehm-ohs 'ahm-breh
Tengo que comer algo.	_I have to eat something._	'tehn-goh keh koh-'mehr 'ahl-goh
¿Tiene algo para tomar?	_Do you have anything to drink?_	tee-'eh-neh 'ahl-goh 'pah-rah toh-'mahr
¿Hay un café/ una cafetería cerca de aquí?	_Is there a cafe near here?_	'a-ee oohn kah-'feh/'ooh-nah kah-feh-teh-'ree-ah 'sehr-kah deh ah-'kee

¿Me puede recomendar un buen restaurante vegetariano?	*Can you recommend a good vegetarian restaurant?*	meh pooh-ʹeh-deh rreh-koh-mehn-ʹdahr oohn booh-ʹehn rehs-tah-ooh-ʹrahn-teh beh-heh-tah-ree-ʹah-noh
¿Dónde está la panadería más cercana?	*Where is the nearest pastry shop?*	ʹdohn-deh ehs-ʹtah lah pah-nah-deh-ʹree-ah mahs sehr-ʹkah-nah
¿Dónde se puede comer barato?	*Where can you go for cheap food?*	ʹdohn-deh seh pooh-ʹeh-deh koh-ʹmehr bah-ʹrah-toh
¿Qué es la comida típica en esta región?	*What's the local specialty?*	keh ehs lah koh-ʹmee-dah ʹtee-pee-kah ehn ʹehs-tah reh-hee-ʹohn

CHAPTER 20: COMIDA EN LA CALLE / STREET FOOD

Listen to Track 31

¿Qué tipo de comida se vende en ese puesto?	_What kind of food is sold at that stand?_	keh 'tee-poh deh koh-'mee-dah seh 'behn-deh ehn 'eh-seh pooh-'ehs-toh
Me da tres tacos de papa, por favor.	_I'd like three potato tacos, please._	meh dah trehs 'tah-kohs deh 'pah-pah, pohr fah-'bvohr
Un vaso chico de..., por favor.	_One small cup/ container of..., please._	oohn 'bah-soh 'chee-koh deh..., pohr fah-'bvohr
Me da un vaso grande de frutas, por favor.	_I'll have one large cup of fruit, please._	meh dah oohn 'bah-soh 'grahn-deh deh 'frooh-tahs, pohr fah-'bvohr
Una orden de papas fritas, por favor.	_One order of french fries, please._	'ooh-nah 'ohr-dehn deh 'pah-pahs 'free-tahs, pohr fah-'bvohr
Sin chile, por favor.	_Without chilli, please._	seen 'chee-leh, pohr fah-'bvohr
Con cebolla.	_With onions._	kohn seh-'boh-yah
¿Qué sabor(es) de... tiene?	_What flavor(s) of... do you have?_	keh sah-'bohr(-ehs) deh... tee-'eh-neh

Listen to Track 32

¿Es picante esta salsa?	_Is this sauce spicy?_	ehs pee-'kahn-teh 'ehs-tah 'sahl-sah
¿Me da un tenedor, por favor?	_Can you give me a fork, please?_	meh dah oohn teh-neh-'dohr, pohr fah-'bvohr
¿Qué tiene hoy?	_What do you have today?_	keh tee-'eh-neh 'oh-ee
¡Qué rico! / ¡Está muy rico!	_It's very tasty._	keh 'rree-koh / ehs-'tah 'mooh-ee 'rree-koh
¿Esto tiene carne? / ¿Esto lleva carne?	_Does this have meat in it?_	'ehs-toh tee-'eh-neh 'kahr-neh / 'ehs-toh 'yeh-bvah 'kahr-neh
¿Qué es esto?	_What's this?_	keh ehs 'ehs-toh
¿Qué tiene para/de tomar?	_What do you have to drink?_	keh tee-'eh-neh 'pah-rah/deh toh-'mahr
¿Qué es eso?	_What's that?_	keh ehs 'eh-soh

CHAPTER 21: EN EL RESTAURANTE / AT THE RESTAURANT

<u>Listen to Track 33</u>

Quisiera reservar una mesa para dos a las nueve.	*I'd like to reserve a table for two for 9 PM.*	kee-see-'eh-rah rreh-sehr-'bvahr 'ooh-nah 'meh-sah 'pah-rah dohs ah lahs nooh-'eh-bveh
¿Cuánto hay que esperar?	*How long do we have to wait?*	kooh-'ahn-toh 'a-ee keh ehs-peh-'rahr
Quisiéramos sentarnos junto a la ventana.	*We would like to sit by the window.*	kee-see-'eh-rah-mohs sehn-'tahr-nohs 'hoon-toh ah lah behn-'tah-nah
¿Tienen una mesa en el área de no fumar?	*Do you have a table in the non-smoking section?*	tee-'eh-nehn 'ooh-nah 'meh-sah ehn ehl 'ah-reh-ah deh noh fooh-'mahr
¿Tienen alguna mesa para esta noche?	*Do you have any tables available for this evening?*	tee-'eh-nehn ahl-'gooh-nah 'meh-sah 'pah-rah 'ehs-tah 'noh-cheh
¿Se puede fumar aquí?	*Can I smoke here?*	seh pooh-'eh-deh fooh-'mahr ah-'kee

¿Me trae un cenicero, por favor?	Can you bring me an ashtray, please?	meh 'trah-eh oohn seh-nee-'seh-roh, pohr fah-'bvohr
¿La cuenta incluye la propina?	Is the tip included in the bill?	lah kooh-'ehn-tah een-'klooh-yeh lah proh-'pee-nah
Nos trae la cuenta, por favor.	Bring us the bill/check, please.	nohs 'trah-eh lah kooh-'ehn-tah, pohr fah-'bvohr
¿Aceptan tarjetas de crédito?	Do you accept credit cards?	ah-'sehp-tahn tahr-'heh-tahs deh 'kreh-dee-toh

CHAPTER 22: PIDIENDO COMIDA Y BEBIDA / ORDERING FOOD AND DRINKS

Listen to Track 34

¿Tiene un menú en inglés?	_Do you have a menu in English?_	tee-'eh-neh oohn meh-'nooh ehn een-'glehs
¿Qué recomienda?	_What do you recommend?_	keh rreh-koh-mee-'ehn-dah
¿Tienen menú infantil?	_Do you have children's meals?_	tee-'eh-nehn meh-'nooh een-fahn-'teel
¿Qué tiene ese platillo?	_What's in that dish?_	keh tee-'eh-neh 'eh-seh plah-'tee-yoh
¿Qué sirven de desayuno?	_What do you have/serve for breakfast?_	keh 'seer-bvehn deh deh-sah-'yooh-noh
Dos órdenes / Una orden	_Two orders / One order_	dohs 'ohr-deh-nehs / 'ooh-nah ohr-dehn
Quisiera una orden de chiles rellenos, por favor.	_I'd like one order of chiles rellenos, please._	kee-see-'eh-rah 'ooh-nah 'ohr-dehn deh 'chee-lehs rreh-'yeh-nohs, pohr fah-'bvohr
Lo quiero bien cocido.	_I'd like it well done._	loh kee-'eh-roh bee-'ehn koh-'see-doh

Quisiera verduras a la parrilla aparte, por favor.	*I would like grilled vegetables on the side.*	kee-see-'eh-rah behr-'dooh-rahs ah lah pah-'rree-yah ah-'pahr-teh, pohr fah-'bvohr

Listen to Track 35

Dos jugos naturales.	*Two juices (freshly squeezed)*	dohs 'hooh-gohs nah-tooh-'rah-lehs
Dos ensaladas.	*Two salads.*	dohs ehn-sah-'lah-dahs
¿Con qué se acompaña?	*What does it come with?*	kohn keh seh ah-kohm-'pah-nyah
¿Qué me recomienda de postre?	*What would you recommend for dessert?*	keh meh rreh-koh-mee-'ehn-dah deh 'pohs-treh
Una copa de vino tinto, por favor.	*One glass of red wine, please.*	'ooh-nah 'koh-pah deh 'bee-noh 'teen-toh, pohr fah-'bvohr
Seco	*Dry*	seh-koh
Quisiera una botella de vino blanco, por favor.	*I would like a bottle of white wine, please.*	kee-see-'eh-rah 'ooh-nah boh-'teh-yah deh 'bee-noh 'blahn-koh, pohr fah-'bvohr
Agua natural con limón, por favor.	*(Still) water with lemon, please.*	'ah-gooh-ah nah-tooh-'rahl kohn lee-'mohn, pohr fah-'bvohr

Un agua mineral sin hielo, por favor.	*Mineral water without ice, please.*	oohn 'ah-gooh-ah mee-neh-'rahl seen ee-'eh-loh, pohr fah-'bvohr
¿Tiene jugo de naranja natural?	*Do you have fresh orange juice?*	tee-'eh-neh 'hooh-goh deh nah-'rahn-hah nah-tooh-'rahl

Listen to Track 36

Un vaso de jugo de naranja, por favor.	*A glass of orange juice, please.*	oohn 'bah-soh deh 'hooh-goh dch nah-'rahn-hah, pohr fah-'bvohr
Un té verde, por favor.	*Green tea, please.*	oohn teh 'behr-deh, pohr fah-'bvohr
Un té helado, por favor.	*Iced tea, please.*	oohn teh eh-'lah-doh, pohr fah-'bvohr
¿Qué cervezas tienen en botellas?	*What bottled beers do you have?*	keh sehr-'bveh-sahs tee-'eh-nehn ehn boh-'teh-yahs
¿Cuánto cuesta una botella?	*How much is a bottle?*	kooh-'ahn-toh kooh-'ehs-tah 'ooh-nah boh-'teh-yah
Me lo trae en un vaso, por favor.	*Bring it to me in a glass, please.*	meh loh 'trah-eh ehn oohn 'bah-soh, pohr fah-'bvohr

Un café chico, con leche, por favor.	*Small coffee with milk, please.*	oohn kah-'feh 'chee-koh, kohn 'leh-cheh, pohr fah-'bvohr
Este café no está caliente. ¿Me lo podría calentar?	*This coffee is not hot. Can you heat it up please?*	'ehs-teh kah-'feh noh ehs-'tah kah-lee-'ehn-teh. Meh loh poh-'dree-ah kah-lehn-'tahr

CHAPTER 23: SALIR DE FIESTA / GOING OUT (PARTYING)

Listen to Track 37

¿Hay algún buen bar cerca de aquí?	*Is there a good bar around here?*	'a-ee ahl-'goohn booh-'ehn bahr 'sehr-kah deh ah-'kee
Vamos a la disco/al antro.	*Let's go to a club.*	'bah-mohs ah lah 'dees-koh/ahl 'ahn-troh
Un bar de moda	*A fashionable/ trendy bar*	oohn bahr deh 'moh-dah
¿Cuánto cuesta el cover?	*What's the cover charge?*	kooh-'ahn-toh kooh-'ehs-tah ehl 'koh-bvehr
Es gratis.	*It's free.*	ehs 'grah-tees
¿Por qué no podemos entrar?	*Why can't we go in?*	pohr keh noh poh-'deh-mohs ehn-'trahr
Yo invito.	*It's on me. / It's my treat.*	yoh een-'bee-toh
¿Qué quieres tomar?	*What would you like to drink?*	keh kee-'eh-rehs toh-'mahr
¿Cuánto?	*How much?*	kooh-'ahn-toh
¡Me encanta este lugar!	*I love this place!*	meh ehn-'kahn-tah 'ehs-teh looh-'gahr
No me gusta este lugar.	*I don't like this place.*	noh meh 'goos-tah 'ehs-teh looh-'gahr

Vamos a otro lugar.	*Let's go somewhere else.*	'bah-mohs ah 'oh-troh looh-'gahr
Quisiera un shot de tequila, por favor.	*I would like a shot of tequila, please.*	kee-see-'eh-rah oohn shot deh teh-'kee-lah, pohr fah-'bvohr
Otra igual, por favor.	*The same, please.*	'oh-trah ee-gooh-'ahl, pohr fah-'bvohr
Estoy borracho.	*I'm drunk.*	ehs-'toh-ee boh-'rrah-choh

PART 7: DE COMPRAS / SHOPPING

CHAPTER 24: NOMBRES DE TIENDAS / STORE NAMES

Listen to Track 38

Una farmacia	*A pharmacy*	ˈooh-nah fahr-ˈmah-see-ah
Una librería	*A bookstore*	ˈooh-nah lee-breh-ˈree-ah
Un almacén	*A department store*	oohn ahl-mah-ˈsehn
Una panadería	*A bakery*	ˈooh-nah pah-nah-deh-ˈree-ah
Una tienda de ropa	*A clothing store*	ˈooh-nah tee-ˈehn-dah deh ˈrroh-pah
Una tienda de comestibles	*A grocery store*	ˈooh-nah tee-ˈehn-dah deh koh-mehs-ˈtee-blehs
Un supermercado	*A supermarket*	oohn sooh-pehr-mehr-ˈkah-doh
Una zapatería	*A shoe store*	ˈooh-nah sah-pah-teh-ˈree-ah
Una ferretería	*A hardware store*	ˈooh-nah feh-rreh-teh-ˈree-ah
Una tienda de regalos	*A gift shop*	ˈooh-nah tee-ˈehn-dah deh rreh-ˈgah-lohs
Una florería	*A florist*	ˈooh-nah floh-reh-ˈree-ah
Una joyería	*A jewelry store*	ˈooh-nah hoh-yeh-ˈree-ah

Un puesto de periódicos	*A news stand*	oohn pooh-'ehs-toh deh peh-ree-'oh-dee-kohs
Una juguetería	*A toy store*	'ooh-nah hooh-geh-teh-'ree-ah

CHAPTER 25: EN EL CENTRO COMERCIAL / AT THE MALL

Listen to Track 39

¿Quiere envolverlo?	*Will you wrap it?*	kee-'eh-reh ehn-bohl-'bvehr-loh
Me lo llevo.	*I'll take it.*	meh loh 'yeh-bvoh
Eso es todo por ahora.	*That's all I want for now.*	'eh-soh ehs 'toh-doh pohr ah-'oh-rah
¿Cómo quiere pagar?	*How do you want to pay?*	'koh-moh kee-'eh-reh pah-'gahr
¿Tienes cambio?	*Do you have change?*	tee-'eh-nehs 'kahm-bee-oh
Busco ...	*I am looking for ...*	'boohs-koh
¿Cuánto es?	*How much is it?*	kooh-'ahn-toh ehs
Por favor muéstreme.	*Please show me.*	pohr fah-'bvohr mooh-'ehs-treh-meh
Aquí está.	*Here it is.*	ah-'kee ehs-'tah
Necesito un intérprete.	*I need an interpreter.*	neh-seh-'see-toh oohn een-'tehr-preh-teh
¿Hay alguien aquí que hable inglés?	*Does anyone here speak English?*	'a-ee 'ahl-gee-ehn ah-'kee keh 'ah-bleh een-'glehs
¿Puede ayudarme, por favor?	*Can you help me, please?*	pooh-'eh-deh ah-yooh-'dahr-meh, pohr fah-'bvohr

Listen to Track 40

No me gusta.	*I don't like it.*	noh meh ˈgoohs-tah
Solo estoy mirando/Estoy bien.	*I'm just looking.*	ˈsoh-loh ehs-ˈtoh-ee mee-ˈrahn-doh/ehs-ˈtoh-ee bee-ˈehn
¿Cuánto cuesta esta camiseta?	*How much does this t-shirt cost?*	koo-ˈahn-toh koo-ˈehs-tah ˈehs-tah kah-mee-ˈseh-tah
¿Me lo puedo probar?	*Can I try it on?*	meh loh pooh-ˈeh-doh proh-ˈbvahr
Es demasiado chico.	*It's too small.*	ehs deh-mah-see-ˈah-doh ˈchee-koh
No me queda bien.	*It doesn't fit.*	noh meh ˈkeh-dah bee-ˈehn
¿Tiene talla grande?	*Do you have large size?*	tee-ˈeh-neh ˈtah-yah ˈgrahn-deh
¿Tienen estos zapatos en número diez (cuarenta y cuatro)?	*Do you have these shoes in size 10 (44)?*	tee-ˈeh-neh ˈehs-tohs sah-ˈpah-tohs ehn ˈnooh-meh-roh dee-ˈehs (koo-ah-ˈrehn-tah ee kooh-ˈah-troh)
Es demasiado caro.	*It's too expensive.*	ehs deh-mah-see-ˈah-doh ˈkah-roh
¿Tiene algo más barato?	*Do you have something cheaper?*	tee-ˈeh-neh ˈahl-goh mahs bah-ˈrah-toh

Hay muchas rebajas aquí.	*There are a lot of specials here.*	ˈa-ee ˈmooh-chahs rreh-ˈbvah-hahs ah-ˈkee
Quisiera devolverlo.	*I would like to return it.*	kee-see-ˈeh-rah deh-bvohl-ˈbvehr-loh

CHAPTER 26: EN EL SUPERMERCADO / AT THE SUPERMARKET

Listen to Track 41

¿Dónde está el supermercado más cercano?	*Where is the nearest supermarket?*	ˈdohn-deh ehs-ˈtah ehl sooh-pehr-mehr-ˈkah-doh mahs sehr-ˈkah-noh
¿En qué pasillo están las sopas instantáneas?	*In which aisle are the instant soups?*	ehn keh pah-ˈsee-yoh ehs-ˈtahn lahs ˈsoh-pahs eens-tahn-ˈtah-neh-ahs
¿Dónde está la sección de lácteos?	*Where is the dairy section?*	ˈdohn-deh ehs-ˈtah lah sehk-see-ˈohn deh ˈlahk-teh-ohs
¿Está tierno/ fresco el pan?	*Is this bread fresh?*	ehs-ˈtah tee-ˈehr-noh/ˈfrehs-koh ehl pahn
¿Cuánto cuesta un kilo de tomates?	*How much is a kilo of tomatoes?*	kooh-ˈahn-toh kooh-ˈehs-tah oohn ˈkee-loh deh toh-ˈmah-tehs
¿Tiene otros tipos de té?	*Do you have other kinds of tea?*	tee-ˈeh-neh ˈoh-trohs ˈtee-pohs deh teh
Quisiera diez rebanadas de este queso.	*I would like 10 slices of this cheese.*	kee-see-ˈeh-rah dee-ˈehs rreh-bah-ˈnah-dahs deh ˈehs-teh ˈkeh-soh

Un poco más.	*A little bit more.*	oohn 'poh-koh mahs
¿Dónde está el lector de precios?	*Where is the price scanner?*	'dohn-deh ehs-'tah ehl lehk-'tohr deh 'preh-see-ohs
¿Podría darme una bolsa, por favor?	*Can you give me a bag, please?*	poh-'dree-ah 'dahr-meh 'ooh-nah 'bohl-sah, pohr fah-'bvohr
No tengo cambio.	*I don't have change.*	noh 'tehn-goh 'kahm-bee-oh

CHAPTER 27: EN LA FARMACIA / AT THE PHARMACY

Listen to Track 42

Necesito algo para la diarrea.	*I need something for diarrhea.*	neh-seh-´see-toh ´ahl-goh ´pah-rah lah dee-ah-´rreh-ah
Leve	*Light (not severe)*	´leh-bveh
Grave	*Serious*	´grah-bveh
¿Cuántas veces al/por día debo tomarlo?	*How many times a day do I take it?*	kooh-´anh-tahs ´beh-sehs ahl/pohr ´dee-ah deh-bvoh toh-´mahr-loh
Una caja/un paquete de curitas	*A box/package of band-aids*	´ooh-nah ´kah-hah/oohn pah-´keh-teh deh kooh-´ree-tahs
¿Tienen algo para las picaduras de mosquitos?	*Do you have anything for mosquito bites?*	tee-´eh-neh ´ahl-goh ´pah-rah lahs pee-kah-´dooh-rahs deh mohs-´kee-tohs
¿En qué sección están las toallas sanitarias?	*What section are your sanitary pads in?*	ehn keh sehk-see-´ohn ehs-´tahn lahs toh-´ah-yahs sah-nee-´tah-ree-ahs
Busco toallas húmedas (anti-bacteriales).	*I'm looking for (anti-bacterial) moist wipes.*	boohs-koh to-´ah-yahs ´ooh-meh-dahs (ahn-tee-bahk-teh-ree-´ah-lehs)

¿Cuánto cuesta el repelente contra mosquitos?	How much is the anti-mosquito spray?	kooh-'ahn-toh kooh-'ehs-tah ehl rreh-peh-'lehn-teh 'kohn-trah mohs-'kee-tohs
¿Es seguro para niños?	Is it safe for kids?	ehs seh-'gooh-roh 'pah-rah 'nee-nyohs
¿Hay filtro solar?	Do you sell sunblock?	'a-ee 'feel-troh soh-'lahr
¿Hay alcohol antiséptico?	Do you sell rubbing alcohol?	'a-ee ahl-koh-'ohl ahn-tee-'sehp-tee-koh
Palillos de algodón	Q-tips	pah-'lee-yohs deh ahl-goh-'dohn

PART 8: SALUD Y BIENESTAR / HEALTH AND WELLNESS

Listen to Track 43

¿Dónde está el hospital más cercano?	*Where is the nearest hospital?*	ˈdohn-deh ehs-ˈtah ehl ohs-pee-ˈtahl mahs sehr-ˈkah-noh
No tengo seguro médico.	*I don't have health insurance.*	noh ˈtehn-goh seh-ˈgooh-roh ˈmeh-dee-koh
¿Podría ver a un doctor que hable inglés?	*Can I see a doctor who speaks English?*	poh-ˈdree-ah behr ah oohn dohk-ˈtohr keh ah-bleh een-ˈglehs
Me picó algún bicho.	*Some insect bit me.*	meh pee-ˈkoh ahl-ˈgoohn ˈbee-choh
¿Podría recetarme algo para la diarrea?	*Can you prescribe something for diarrhea?*	poh-ˈdree-ah rre-seh-ˈtahr-meh ˈahl-goh ˈpah-rah lah dee-ah-ˈrre-ah
¿Con qué frecuencia debo tomarlo?	*How often do I have to take it?*	kohn keh freh-kooh-ˈehn-see-ah ˈdeh-bvoh toh-ˈmahr-loh
El medicamento	*Medicine*	ehl meh-dee-kah-ˈmehn-toh
Soy alérgico a la penicilina.	*I'm allergic to penicillin.*	ˈsoh-ee ah-ˈlehr-hee-koh ah lah peh-nee-see-ˈlee-nah

Soy alérgico a las abejas.	*I'm allergic to bees.*	'soh-ee ah-'lehr-hee-koh ah lahs ah-'bveh-hahs
Mi rodilla está hinchada.	*My knee is swollen.*	mee rroh-'dee-yah ehs-'tah een-'chah-dah
No puedo mover mi brazo.	*I can't move my arm.*	noh pooh-'eh-doh moh-'bvehr mee 'brah-soh

Listen to Track 44

Me duele el estómago.	*My stomach hurts.*	meh dooh-'eh-leh ehl ehs-'toh-mah-goh
Tengo fiebre.	*I have a fever.*	'tehn-goh fee-'eh-breh
Tengo nauseas.	*I feel nauseous.*	'tehn-goh 'nah-ooh-seh-ahs
He estado vomitando.	*I've been vomiting.*	eh ehs-'tah-doh bo-mee-'tahn-doh
Tengo dolor de cabeza.	*I have a headache.*	'tehn-goh doh-'lohr deh kah-'bveh-sah
Me siento mareado.	*I feel dizzy.*	meh see-'ehn-toh mah-reh-'ah-doh
Me siento destemplado.	*I feel slightly feverish.*	meh see-'ehn-toh dehs-tehm-'plah-doh
Me siento así desde hace dos días.	*I've been feeling like this for two days.*	meh see-'ehn-toh ah-'see 'dehs-deh 'ah-seh dohs 'dee-ahs

Tengo un dolor de muelas.	*I have a toothache.*	ˈtehn-goh oohn doh-ˈlohr deh mooh-ˈeh-lahs
Se me cayó una amalgama.	*I lost a filling.*	seh meh kah-ˈyoh ˈooh-nah ah-mahl-ˈgah-mah
¿Me dará sueño?	*Will it make me drowsy?*	meh dah-ˈrah sooh-ˈeh-nyoh

CHAPTER 29: SEGURIDAD / SAFETY

Listen to Track 45

Perdí mi cartera.	*I lost my wallet.*	pehr-ˈdee mee kahr-ˈteh-rah
Por aquí.	*Somewhere around here.*	pohr ah-ˈkee
Alguien robó mi cartera.	*Someone stole my wallet.*	ahl-gee-ˈehn rroh-ˈboh mee kahr-ˈteh-rah
¿Alguien devolvió una cartera?	*Has anyone returned a wallet?*	ahl-gee-ˈehn deh-bvohl-bvee-ˈoh ˈooh-nah kahr-ˈteh-rah
Aquí tiene mi número. Por favor llámeme si la encuentra.	*Here's my number. Please call me if you find it.*	ah-ˈkee tee-ˈeh-neh mee ˈnooh-meh-roh. pohr fah-ˈbvohr ˈya-meh-meh see lah ehn-kooh-ˈehn-trah
Se robó mi cámara.	*My camera was stolen.*	seh rroh-ˈboh mee ˈkah-mah-rah
Se robó mi mochila.	*My backpack was stolen.*	seh rroh-ˈboh mee moh-ˈchee-lah
Llame a la policía.	*Call the police.*	ˈyah-meh ah lah poh-lee-ˈsee-ah
¡Ladrón!	*Thief!*	lah-ˈdrohn
¡Pare!	*Stop!*	ˈpah-reh

¿Me podría ayudar, por favor?	*Could you help me, please?*	meh poh-'dree-ah ah-yooh-'dahr, pohr fah-'bvohr
Estoy perdido.	*I'm lost.*	ehs-'toh-ee pehr-'dee-doh
Ya no tengo dinero.	*I don't have any money left.*	yah noh 'tehn-goh dee-'neh-roh

PART 9: AUTORIDAD / AUTHORITY

Listen to Track 46

No he hecho nada malo.	*I haven't done anything wrong.*	noh eh ˈeh-choh ˈnah-dah ˈmah-loh
Por favor, hubo un malentendido.	*Please, there has been a mistake.*	pohr fah-ˈbvohr, ˈooh-bvoh oohn mahl-ehn-tehn-ˈdee-doh
Fue un malentendido.	*It was a mis-understanding.*	fooh-ˈeh oohn mahl-ehn-tehn-ˈdee-doh
¿Adónde me lleva?	*Where are you taking me?*	ah-ˈdohn-deh meh ˈyeh-bvah
¿Estoy arrestado/a?	*Am I under arrest?*	ehs-ˈtoh-ee ah-rrehs-ˈtah-doh/ ah
Quiero hablar con un abogado.	*I want to talk to a lawyer.*	kee-ˈeh-roh ah-ˈblahr kohn oohn ah-bvoh-ˈgah-doh
¿Puedo pagar la multa ahora?	*Can I just pay a fine now?*	pooh-ˈeh-doh pah-ˈgar lah ˈmoohl-tah ah-ˈoh-rah
Yo confieso.	*I confess.*	yoh con-fi-ˈeh-soh

PART 10: FRASES CONVERSACIONALES / CONVERSATIONAL PHRASES

Listen to Track 47

Estoy estupen-damente.	*I'm feeling fantastic.*	ehs-'toh-ee ehs-tooh-pehn-dah-'mehn-teh
No podría estar mejor.	*I couldn't be better.*	noh poh-'dree-ah ehs-'tahr meh-'hohr
Efectivamente.	*That's right. / Exactly right.*	eh-fehk-tee-bvah-'mehn-teh
Lo que pasa es que...	*The thing is that...*	loh keh 'pah-sah ehs keh
Se podría decir que...	*One could say that... / It could be said that...*	seh poh-'dree-ah deh-'seer keh
¡No seas pesado!	*Don't be a pain!*	noh 'seh-ahs peh-'sah-doh
¡Eres un plasta!	*You're a pain!*	'eh-rehs oohn 'plahs-tah
Es decir que...	*In other words...*	ehs deh-'seer keh
Digamos que...	*Let's say that...*	dee-'gah-mohs keh
No me mientas.	*Don't lie to me.*	noh meh mee-'ehn-tahs
Lo que más me gusta es...	*The thing I like most is...*	loh keh mahs meh 'goohs-tah ehs
¡Qué casualidad!	*What a coincidence!*	keh kah-sooh-ah-lee-'dahd
Hasta altas horas.	*Until the early hours.*	'ahs-tah 'ahl-tahs 'oh-rahs

Listen to Track 48

Estoy molido.	*I'm beat (crushed).*	'ehs-toh-ee moh-'lee-doh
Estoy hecho polvo.	*I'm beat (ground to dust).*	ehs-'toh-ee 'eh-choh 'pohl-bvoh
Me lo imagino.	*I can imagine.*	meh loh ee-mah-'hee-noh
Aparte de ser...	*Apart from being...*	ah-'pahr-teh deh sehr
Pongámonos en marcha.	*Let's get going. / Let's get moving.*	pohn-'gah-moh-nohs ehn 'mahr-chah
A mi ver...	*In my opinion... / In my view...*	ah mee 'behr
Más allá	*Beyond*	mahs ah-'yah
Con tal de que...	*Provided that... / As long as...*	kohn tahl deh keh
Estoy a punto de...	*I'm about to...*	ehs-'toh-ee ah 'poohn-toh deh
¿Cómo que...?	*What do you mean that...?*	'koh-moh keh
¿Cuánto tiempo llevas (gerundio)?	*How long have you been (doing something)?*	kooh-'ahn-toh tee-'ehm-poh 'yeh-bvahs
¿Es verdad esto de que...?	*Is it true (what I've heard) that...?*	ehs behr-'dahd 'ehs-toh deh keh
¿Cuánto tiempo llevas aquí?	*How long have you been here?*	kooh-'ahn-toh tee-'ehm-poh 'yeh-bvahs ah-'kee

Listen to Track 49

Sobre gustos no hay nada escrito.	To each his own. (Literally: Regarding taste, nothing is written.)	'soh-breh 'goohs-tohs noh 'a-ee 'nah-dah ehs-'kree-toh
Ya basta de...	Enough of... / Enough with...	yah 'bahs-tah deh
Me han dicho que...	I have been told that... / They have told me that...	meh ahn 'dee-choh keh
Tiene (algo) que ver con...	It has (something) to do with...	tee-'eh-neh keh behr kohn
Ya veremos.	We'll see.	yah beh-'reh-mohs
Mientras tanto,...	Meanwhile,... / In the meantime,...	mee-'ehn-trahs 'tahn-toh
Tengo (muchas) ganas de...	I (really) feel like... / I (really) look forward to...	'tehn-goh ('mooh-chahs) 'gah-nahs deh
Ser capaz de...	To be able to... / To be capable of...	sehr kah-'pahs deh
Lo que más espero es...	What I hope most is...	lo keh mahs ehs-'peh-roh ehs
Tienes (toda la) razón.	You are (completely) correct.	tee-'eh-nehs ('toh-dah lah) rrah-'sohn
Lo tengo muy claro.	It's very clear to me.	loh 'tehn-goh 'mooh-ee 'klah-roh
Me muero de ganas de...	I am dying to...	meh mooh-'eh-roh deh 'gah-nahs deh

Listen to Track 50

Estamos de vuelta.	*We're back.*	ehs-'tah-mohs deh booh-'ehl-tah
Te hará bien...	*It will do you good to...*	teh ah-'rah bee-'ehn
La verdad es que...	*The truth is that...*	lah behr-'dahd ehs keh
¡Está hecho un desastre!	*It's a mess!*	ehs-'tah 'eh-choh oohn deh-'sahs-treh
Por última vez	*For the last time*	pohr 'oohl-tee-mah 'behs
No me emociona(n)...	*I'm not thrilled about... / I don't get excited about...*	noh meh eh-moh-see-'oh-nah(n)
¿Qué me dices?	*What are you saying? / What are you telling me?*	keh meh 'dee-sehs
¡No me digas!	*You don't say! / Don't tell me! / Well I never!*	noh meh 'dee-gahs
Estoy de acuerdo (contigo).	*I agree (with you).*	ehs-'toh-ee deh ah-kooh-'ehr-doh (kohn-'tee-goh)
No está nada mal.	*That's not bad at all.*	noh ehs-'tah 'nah-dah mahl
Me di cuenta de que...	*I realized that...*	meh dee kooh-'ehn-tah deh keh
Me pilló desprevenido.	*It caught me off guard.*	meh pee-'yoh dehs-preh-bveh-'nee-doh

Listen to Track 51

Punto final.	Period. / The end.	'poohn-toh fee-'nahl
No tengo ni idea.	I have no idea.	noh 'tehn-goh nee ee-'deh-ah
Te lo prometo.	I promise you.	teh loh proh-'meh-toh
¿Tienes fuego?	Got a light? (Literally: Do you have fire?)	tee-'eh-nehs fooh-'eh-goh
¿Me das fuego?	Got a light? (Literally: Will you give me fire?)	meh dahs fooh-'eh-goh
Me defiendo bastante bien.	I get by pretty well.	meh deh-fee-'ehn-doh bahs-'tahn-teh bee-'ehn
Me las apaño muy bien.	I manage very well.	meh lahs ah-'pah-neeh-oh 'mooh-eh bee-'ehn
(No) tengo derecho a...	I (don't) have the right to...	noh 'tehn-goh deh-'reh-choh ah...
Si yo dijera que...	If I said that... / If I were to say that...	see yoh dee-'heh-rah keh...
Por un lado... y por otro lado...	On one hand... and on the other hand...	pohr oohn 'lah-doh... ee pohr 'oh-troh 'lah-doh
Al contrario	On the contrary	ahl kohn-'trah-ree-oh
Deberías tomar ejemplo de...	You should follow the example of...	deh-beh-'ree-ahs toh-'mahr eh-'hehm-ploh deh...

Listen to Track 52

¿Cómo diría yo?	*How should I say it? / How can I put it?*	ˈkoh-moh dee-ˈree-ah yoh
No te enfades.	*Don't get angry.*	noh teh ehn-ˈfah-dehs
No te lo tomes (a) mal.	*Don't take it the wrong way.*	noh teh loh ˈtoh-mehs (ah) mahl
¡Qué mala pata!	*What bad luck! / What rotten luck!*	keh ˈmah-lah ˈpah-tah
¡Ponte en fila!	*Get in line! / Line up!*	ˈpohn-teh ehn ˈfee-lah
Eso sí que es verdad.	*That is indeed true. / That, yes, is true.*	ˈeh-so see keh ehs behr-ˈdahd
Me cuesta mucho...	*I find it difficult to...*	meh kooh-ˈehs-tah ˈmooh-choh...
Con respecto a...	*With respect to... / As far as (X) is concerned...*	kohn rrehs-ˈpehk-toh ah
La intención es lo que cuenta.	*It's the thought that counts.*	lah een-tehn-see-ˈohn ehs loh keh kooh-ˈehn-tah
Dame el beneficio de la duda.	*Give me the benefit of the doubt.*	ˈdah-meh ehl beh-neh-ˈfee-see-oh deh lah ˈdooh-dah
Vamos a por ello.	*Let's get to it. / Let's go for it.*	ˈbah-mohs ah pohr ˈeh-yoh
A primera hora de la mañana.	*First thing in the morning.*	ah pree-ˈmeh-rah ˈoh-rah deh lah mah-ˈnyah-nah

Listen to Track 53

¿Qué te pasa?	_What's the matter?_	keh teh ˈpah-sah
Soy un desastre en... / No tengo esperanza en...	_I'm hopeless at..._	ˈsoh-ee oohn deh-ˈsahs-treh ehn/ noh ˈtehn-goh ehs-peh-ˈrahn-sah ehn
¡Estás para comerte!	_You look fantastic! / You look good enough to eat!_	ehs-ˈtahs ˈpah-rah koh-ˈmehr-teh
¡Estás más bueno que el pan!	_You look fantastic! / You look scrumptious!_	ehs-ˈtahs mahs booh-ˈeh-noh keh ehl pahn
Me lo he pasado (muy) bien.	_I had a (very) good time. / I have had a (very) good time._	meh loh eh pah-ˈsah-doh (ˈmooh-ee) bee-ˈehn
En resumen,...	_In summary,..._	ehn rreh-ˈsooh-mehn
Sin duda	_Without a doubt, undoubtedly_	seen ˈdooh-dah
Está muy bien hecho.	_It is very well done/made._	ehs-ˈtah ˈmooh-ee bee-ˈehn ˈeh-choh
Estoy de mal humor.	_I'm in a bad mood._	ehs-ˈtoh-ee deh mahl ooh-ˈmohr
Apesta a...	_It reeks of..._	ah-ˈpehs-tah ah
Eres un plomo.	_You are boring. / You are a bore._	ˈeh-rehs oohn ˈploh-moh
Mejor dicho,...	_Rather,... / Better said,..._	meh-ˈhohr ˈdee-choh

89

Listen to Track 54

Que en paz descanse.	*May God rest his/her soul.*	keh ehn pahs dehs-'kahn-seh
No tiene gracia.	*It's not funny.*	noh tee-'eh-neh 'grah-see-ah
Eso no lo sabía yo.	*I did not know that. / That I didn't know.*	'eh-soh noh loh sah-'bvee-ah yoh
Te toca a ti.	*Your turn. / It's your turn.*	teh 'toh-kah ah tee
Me toca a mí.	*My turn. / It's my turn.*	meh 'toh-kah ah mee
¿Te apetece...?	*Do you fancy...? / Would you like to...?*	teh ah-peh-'teh-seh
¿Tienes ganas de...?	*Do you feel like...? / Are you up for...?*	tee-'eh-nehs 'gah-nahs deh
Espero que lo pases (muy) bien.	*I hope you have a (very) good time.*	ehs-'peh-roh keh loh 'pah-sehs 'mooh-ee bee-'ehn
Hasta la próxima.	*Until next time.*	'ahs-tah lah 'prohk-seeh-mah
Eso no me suena.	*That doesn't ring a bell.*	'eh-soh noh meh sooh-'eh-nah
De vez en cuando	*From time to time / once in awhile*	deh behs ehn kooh-'ahn-doh
Me alegro (mucho) de que...	*I am (really) glad that...*	meh ah-'leh-groh ('mooh-choh) deh keh...

Listen to Track 55

¿Cómo te encuentras ahora?	_How do you feel now? / How are you feeling now?_	'koh-moh teh ehn-kooh-'ehn-trahs ah-'oh-rah
Como por ejemplo...	_For example..._	'koh-moh pohr eh-'hehm-ploh...
Hasta cierto punto	_Up to a point / To some extent_	'ahs-tah see-'ehr-toh 'poohn-toh
Tiene lugar en...	_It takes place in... / It occurs in..._	tee-'eh-neh looh-'gahr ehn...
¡Estoy hasta el gorro!	_I've had enough! / I'm fed up! (I'm up to my cap!)_	ehs-'toh-ee 'ahs-tah ehl-'goh-rroh
¡Estoy hasta la coronilla!	_I've had enough! / I'm fed up! (I'm up to my crown!)_	ehs-'toh-ee 'ahs-tah lah koh-roh-'nee-yah
¿Qué opinas de...?	_What do you think about...? / What is your opinion of...?_	keh oh-'pee-nahs deh...
Prefiero que...	_I'd prefer that... / I prefer that..._	preh-fee-'eh-roh keh...
¿Qué haces?	_What are you doing?_	keh 'ah-sehs
Por lo tanto	_Therefore / Hence_	pohr loh 'tahn-toh
¿Es cierto que hay...?	_Is it true that there is/are...?_	ehs see-'ehr-toh keh 'a-ee
¿Cómo te va?	_How's it going?_	'koh-moh teh bah

Listen to Track 56

Es un placer estar aquí.	It's a pleasure to be here.	ehs oohn plah-'sehr ehs-'tahr ah-'kee
¡No me lo puedo creer!	I can't believe it!	noh meh loh pooh-'eh-doh kreh-'ehr
Aunque (algo)... haré (algo diferente) de todos modos.	Although (something)... I'll do (something contrasting) anyway.	a-'oohn-keh ('ahl-goh)... ah-'reh ('ahl-goh dee-feh-'rehn-teh) deh 'toh-dohs 'moh-dohs
¡Eso no te lo crees ni tú!	Not even you believe that!	'eh-soh noh teh loh 'kreh-ehs nee tooh
Cerrada con llave	Locked	seh-'rrah-dah kohn 'yah-bveh
En conjunto,...	All in all,...	ehn kohn-'hoohn-toh
Al día siguiente	The next day / The following day	ahl 'dee-ah see-gee-'ehn-teh
No tengo la impresión de que...	I don't have the impression that... / I don't have the feeling that...	noh 'tehn-goh lah eehm-preh-see-'ohn deh keh
Me parece que...	I think that... / It seems to me that...	meh pah-'reh-seh keh
¿Cómo puede ser que...?	How can it be that...?	'koh-moh pooh-'eh-deh sehr keh...?

No vale la pena.	It's not worth it. / It's not worth the bother.	noh 'bah-leh lah 'peh-nah
Ojalá que sí.	*I hope so.*	oh-hah-'lah keh see
Ojalá que no.	*I hope not.*	oh-hah-'lah keh noh

Listen to Track 57

Tengo (un poco de) miedo.	*I am (a little) scared.*	'tehn-goh (oohn 'poh-koh deh) mee-'eh-doh
Todo va sobre ruedas.	*Everything is fine. / Everything is running smoothly.*	'toh-doh 'bah 'soh-breh rrooh-'eh-dahs
No me había dado cuenta de que...	*I hadn't realized that...*	noh meh ah-'bvee-ah dah-doh kooh-'ehn-tah deh keh
Al final,...	*In the end,...*	ahl fee-'nahl
Si nos quedamos sin (algo)...	*If we run out of (something)...*	see nohs keh-'dah-mohs seen ('ahl-goh)
¡Vete ya!	*Get lost! / Beat it! / Go away!*	'beh-teh yah
¿No te fías de mí?	*Don't you have faith in me?*	noh teh 'fee-ahs deh mee
Es hora de...	*It's time to...*	ehs 'oh-rah deh
¿No confías en mí?	*Don't you trust me?*	noh kohn-'fee-ahs ehn mee

Tiene mala leche.	He/She is bad-tempered. / He/She has bad blood.	tee-'eh-neh 'mah-lah 'leh-cheh
Está muerto/a de miedo.	He/She is scared to death.	ehs-'tah mooh-'ehr-toh/ah deh mee-'eh-doh
Mejor solo que mal acompañado.	Better (to be) alone than in bad company.	meh-'hohr 'soh-loh keh mahl ah-kohm-pah-'nyah-doh

Listen to Track 58

Están hablando entre ellos.	They are talking among(st) themselves.	ehs-'tahn ah-'blahn-doh 'ehn-treh 'eh-yohs
Me ha salido un imprevisto.	Something unexpected has come up.	meh ah sah-'lee-doh oohn eem-preh-'bveehs-toh
Es hora de despedirnos.	It's time for us to say goodbye.	ehs 'oh-rah deh dehs-peh-'deehr-nohs
Tengo mucho que contarte.	I've got lots to tell you.	'tehn-goh 'mooh-choh keh kohn-'tahr-teh
Ten calma.	Be calm. / Calm down. / Take it easy.	tehn 'kahl-mah
No te desesperes.	Do not despair.	noh teh deh-sehs-'peh-rehs
De todos modos	Anyway/anyhow	de 'toh-dohs 'moh-dohs
Me parece perfecto.	Seems perfect to me.	meh pah-'reh-seh pehr-'fehk-toh

94

No sé si estoy muy contento.	I don't know if I'm very happy.	noh seh see ehs-'toh-ee 'mooh-ee kohn-'tehn-toh
Eso nos pasa a todos.	That happens to us all. / That happens to everyone.	'eh-soh nohs 'pah-sah ah 'toh-dohs
¿Qué tal el fin de semana?	How was your weekend?	keh tahl ehl feehn deh seh-'mah-nah
Tengo pendiente...	I have yet to...	'tehn-goh pehn-dee-'ehn-teh

Listen to Track 59

¡Qué guay!	How cool!	keh gooh-'a-ee
Como he dicho,...	As I have said,...	'koh-moh eh 'dee-choh
Todos lo hemos hecho.	We've all done it.	'toh-dohs loh 'eh-mohs 'eh-choh
Tengo unas ganas locas de...	I have a mad desire to...	'tehn-goh 'ooh-nahs 'gah-nahs 'loh-kahs deh
Eso no es mala idea.	That's not a bad idea.	'eh-soh noh ehs 'mah-lah ee-'deh-ah
Eso es una buena manera de decirlo.	That's a good way to say it. / That's a good way to put it.	'eh-soh ehs 'ooh-nah booh'eh-nah mah-'nehr-ah deh deh-'seer-loh
El hecho de que...	The fact that...	ehl 'eh-choh deh keh

¿Adónde podemos ir a picotear algo?	Where can we go for a bite to eat?	ah-ˈdohn-deh poh-ˈdeh-mohs eehr ah pee-koh-teh-ˈahr ˈahl-goh
¿Adónde podemos ir de copas?	Where can we go for a drink?	ah-ˈdohn-deh poh-ˈdeh-mohs eehr deh ˈkoh-pahs
No lo dudaría ni un segundo.	I wouldn't hesitate for a second.	noh loh dooh-dah-ˈree-ah nee oohn seh-ˈgoohn-doh
Sobre todo	Above all / mainly	ˈsoh-breh ˈtoh-doh
Lo especial de (algo) es...	The special thing about (something) is...	loh ehs-peh-see-ˈahl deh (ˈahl-goh) ehs

Listen to Track 60

Hay un corte de luz.	There is a power outage. / There is a blackout.	ˈa-ee oohn ˈkohr-teh deh loohs
¿Puedo pedirte un favor?	Can I ask you a favor?	poohˈeh-doh peh-ˈdeer-teh oohn fah-ˈbvohr
Lo que hemos hecho.	What we have done.	loh keh ˈeh-mohs ˈeh-choh
Ahora mismo vuelvo.	I'll be right back. / Be right back.	ah-ˈoh-rah ˈmees-moh booh-ˈehl-bvoh
No voy a decir nada al respecto.	I won't say anything about it.	noh ˈboh-ee ah deh-ˈseehr ˈnah-dah ahl rehs-ˈpehk-toh

Precio de la entrada por confirmar.	*Ticket/admission price to be confirmed.*	'preh-see-oh deh lah ehn-'trah-dah pohr kohn-feehr-'mahr
Está en la punta de la lengua.	*It's on the tip of my tongue.*	ehs-'tah ehn lah 'poohn-tah deh lah 'lehn-gooh-ah
¿Qué hay de nuevo?	*What's new?*	keh 'a-ee deh nooh-'eh-bvoh
Hoja en blanco	*Blank sheet / Blank page*	'oh-hah ehn 'blahn-koh
Tienes que tener en cuenta que...	*You have to keep in mind that... / You have to take into account that...*	tee-'eh-nehs keh teh-'nehr ehn kooh-'ehn-tah keh
En caso de que...	*In the event that...*	ehn 'kah-soh deh keh
Al cabo de un rato	*After a while / After some time*	ahl 'kah-bvoh deh oohn 'rrah-toh
He cambiado de opinión.	*I've changed my mind.*	eh kahm-bee-'ah-doh deh oh-pee-nee-'ohn

Listen to Track 61

No había más remedio.	*There was no other choice.*	noh ah-'bvee-ah mahs rreh-'meh-dee-oh
Era una tontería...	*It was silly to... / It was foolish to...*	'eh-rah 'ooh-nah tohn-teh-'ree-ah
No podía dejar de...	*I couldn't stop...*	noh poh-'dee-ah deh-'hahr deh

Me dije a mí mismo... / Me dije a mí misma...	*I said to myself... / I told myself...*	meh ˈdee-heh ah mee ˈmeehs-moh / meh ˈdee-heh ah mee ˈmeehs-mah
No soporto que...	*I hate it when... / I can't stand it when...*	noh soh-ˈpohr-toh keh...
¡Ya me acuerdo!	*Now I remember!*	yah meh ah-kooh-ˈehr-doh
Cambiando de tema,...	*To change the subject,... / Moving on,... / On a different note,...*	kahm-bee-ˈahn-doh deh ˈteh-mah
Cogidos de la mano	*Holding hands / hand in hand*	koh-ˈheeh-dohs deh lah ˈmah-noh
Era entonces o nunca.	*It was then or never.*	ˈeh-rah ehn-ˈtohn-sehs oh ˈnoohn-kah
¿Qué tal? (informal) / ¿Como estás? (informal) / ¿Cómo está (usted)? (formal)	*How are you?*	keh tahl / ˈkoh-moh ehs-ˈtahs / ˈkoh-moh ehs-ˈtahs (oohs-ˈtehd)
¿Qué ha pasado?	*What happened? / What has happened?*	keh ah pah-ˈsah-doh
Suele pasar.	*That happens. / That tends to happen.*	sooh-ˈeh-leh pah-ˈsahr

Listen to Track 62

¡Qué sorpresa!	_What a surprise!_	keh sohr-ˈpreh-sah
Adiós a todos.	_Goodbye to all. / Bye everyone._	ah-dee-ˈohs ah ˈtoh-dohs
No me queda otro remedio.	_I have no other choice. / I don't have any other choice._	noh meh ˈkeh-dah ˈoh-troh rreh-ˈmeh-dee-oh
Ten en cuenta que...	_Keep in mind that..._	tehn ehn kooh-ˈehn-tah keh
O, mejor aún...	_Or, even better... / or, better yet..._	oh, meh-ˈhohr ah-ˈoohn
Disculpa las molestias.	_Sorry for the inconvenience._	deehs-ˈkoohl-pah lahs moh-ˈlehs-tee-ahs
¿Te has fijado en que...?	_Have you noticed that...?_	teh ahs fee-ˈhah-doh ehn keh
Acto seguido	_Thereupon / Immediately afterwards_	ˈahk-toh seh-ˈgee-doh
Miré por encima del hombro...	_I looked over my shoulder..._	mee-ˈreh pohr ehn-ˈsee-mah dehl ˈohm-broh
Justamente estábamos hablando de ti.	_We were just talking about you._	hoohs-tah-ˈmehn-teh ehs-ˈtah-bvah-mohs ah-ˈbvlahn-doh deh tee
Me encogí de hombros.	_I shrugged (my shoulders)._	meh ehn-koh-ˈhee deh ˈohm-brohs

Me encargo de eso.	*I'll handle that. / I'll take care of that.*	meh ehn-'kahr-goh deh 'eh-soh
Deja que te cuente que...	*Let me tell you that...*	'deh-hah keh teh kooh'ehn-teh keh...
No obstante,...	*However,...*	noh ohbvs-'tahn-teh

PART 11: FRASES AVANZADAS / ADVANCED PHRASES

Listen to Track 63

La cuenta corriente	*Checking account*	lah kooh'ehn-tah koh-rree-'ehn-teh
Dar la cara	*To take responsibility*	dahr lah 'kah-rah
Marcar la pauta	*To direct / To set the trend*	mahr-'kahr lah 'pah-ooh-tah
El poder adquisitivo	*Purchasing power*	ehl poh-'dehr ahd-kee-see-'tee-bvoh
La segmentación del mercado	*Market segmentation*	lah sehg-mehn-tah-see-'ohn dehl mehr-'kah-doh
Llevar a cabo	*To carry out*	yeh-'bvahr ah 'kah-bvoh
Compra a plazos	*Buy in installments*	'kohm-prah ah 'plah-sohs
Ser osado	*To be risky*	sehr oh-'sah-doh
La participación en el mercado	*Market share*	lah pahr-tee-see-pah-see-'ohn ehn ehl mehr-'kah-doh
Ir al grano	*To get to the point*	eehr ahl 'grah-noh
Ser capaz	*To be able to*	sehr kah-'pahs
La organización sin fines de lucro	*Nonprofit organization*	lah ohr-gah-nee-sah-see-'ohn seen 'fee-nehs deh 'looh-kroh
Estar encargado de...	*To be in charge of... / To have charge of...*	ehs-'tahr ehn-kahr-'gah-doh deh

Listen to Track 64

Dar de baja	*To dismiss or kick out*	dahr deh 'bah-hah
Visita domiciliaria	*Home visit*	bee-'see-tah doh-mee-see-lee-'ah-ree-ah
Tratar con	*To deal with*	trah-'tahr kohn
Estar dispuesto	*To be willing/ prepared/ready (to)*	ehs-'tahr deehs-pooh-'ehs-toh
Aun así	*Even so*	ah-'oohn ah-'see
Tener a la vista	*To have in sight / To have received a letter*	teh-'nehr ah lah 'beehs-tah
A propósito	*By the way*	ah proh-'poh-see-toh
Control de natalidad	*Birth control*	kohn-'trohl deh nah-tah-lee-'dahd
Se solicita	*Wanted*	seh soh-lee-'see-tah
Sacar a plaza / Sacar a la luz	*To bring out into the open or make public what was unknown/hidden*	sah-'kahr ah 'plah-sah / sah-'kahr ah la loohs
Estar de duelo	*To mourn / To be in mourning*	ehs-'tahr deh dooh-'eh-loh
El gusto es mío.	*The pleasure is mine.*	ehl 'goohs-toh ehs 'mee-oh

Listen to Track 65

Ponerse de rodillas	*To kneel*	poh-'nehr-seh deh rroh-'dee-yahs
Tomar tiempo libre	*To take time off*	toh-'mahr tee-'ehm-poh 'lee-breh
Delante de...	*In front of...*	deh-'lahn-teh deh
Hacer favoritismos en prejuicio de...	To show *favoritism to the detriment of...*	ah-'sehr fah-bvoh-ree-'tees-mohs ehn preh-hooh-'ee-see-oh deh
Tener tiempo libre	*To have time off*	teh-'nehr tee-'ehm-poh 'lee-breh
Libro mayor	*Ledger*	'lee-broh mah-'yohr
Por consiguiente	*Consequently / Therefore*	pohr kohn-see-gee-'ehn-teh
Tener la bondad de...	*To be good/kind enough to...*	teh-'nehr lah bohn-'dahd deh
Ya mero	*Very soon / Just about to*	yah 'meh-roh
Está de más.	*It is unnecessary, superfluous.*	ehs-'tah deh mahs
Desde ahora	*From now on*	'dehs-deh ah-'oh-rah
En el futuro	*In the future*	ehn ehl fooh-'tooh-roh
Ya no	*No longer*	yah noh

Listen to Track 66

Papel de seda	*Tissue paper*	pah-'pehl deh 'seh-dah
De seguida	*Continuously / Without interruption / At once*	deh seh-'gee-dah
No que yo sepa	*Not to my knowledge*	noh keh yoh 'seh-pah
Tener en cuenta	*To consider / To take into account*	teh-'nehr ehn kooh-'ehn-tah
Dar fe de	*To vouch for / To testify to*	dahr feh deh
A los pocos meses	*After a few months / Within a few months*	ah lohs 'poh-kohs 'meh-sehs
De canto	*On (its) edge / On its side / Edgewise*	deh 'kahn-toh
La rutina diaria	*The daily grind*	lah rrooh-'tee-nah dee-'ah-ree-ah
A las claras	*Clearly / Frankly / Straight out*	ah lahs 'klah-rahs
Llevar la cuenta	*To keep score or tally (of) / To keep track of*	yeh-'bvahr lah kooh-'ehn-tah
A principios de	*Early in*	ah-preen-'see-pee-ohs deh
A semejanza de...	*In the manner of... / Along the lines of... / Following the example of...*	ah seh-meh-'hahn-sah deh

Listen to Track 67

Pintarle un violín	*To break one's word / To thumb one's nose at / To ignore someone / To tell someone to go to hell (fig.)*	peehn-'tahr-leh oohn bee-oh-'leehn
Razón social	*Business name*	rrah-'sohn soh-see-'ahl
Tomar el sol	*To sunbathe*	toh-'mahr ehl sohl
Poner en razón	*To bring to reason*	poh-'nehr ehn rrah-'sohn
Por ningún motivo	*Under no circumstances / No matter what*	pohr neehn-'goohn moh-'tee-bvoh
De parte de	*On behalf of / In favor of*	deh 'pahr-teh deh
De ahí en adelante	*From then on*	deh ah-'ee ehn ah-deh-'lahn-teh
Perderse de vista	*To vanish / To be lost from view / To drop out of sight*	pehr-'dehr-seh deh 'bees-tah
Tener el pico de oro	*To be eloquent*	teh-'nehr ehl 'pee-koh deh 'oh-roh
Tener la culpa	*To be to blame*	teh-'nehr lah 'koohl-pah
Suceda lo que suceda	*Come what may / No matter what*	sooh-'seh-dah loh keh sooh-'seh-dah

En un improviso	*In a moment*	ehn oohn eem-proh-'bvee-soh
Trastos de cocina	*Kitchen utensils*	'trahs-tohs deh koh-'see-nah

Listen to Track 68

Hacer un pedido	*To place an order*	ah-'sehr oohn peh-'dee-doh
Hacerse uno rajas	*To wear oneself out*	ah-'sehr-seh 'ooh-noh 'rrah-hahs
Ningún otro	*Nobody else / None other*	neehn-'goohn 'oh-troh
Valer la pena	*To be worthwhile*	bah-'lehr lah 'peh-nah
Si no fuera porque	*Except for*	see noh fooh-'eh-rah pohr-'keh
De una pieza	*Solid / Of one piece*	deh 'ooh-nah pee-'eh-sah
Estar de conformidad con	*To be in compliance with*	ehs-'tahr deh kohn-fohr-mee-'dahd kohn
Dar una pasada por	*To pass / Walk by / To take a run at*	dahr 'ooh-nah pah-'sah-dah pohr
Estar en un aprieto	*To be in a jam / To be in trouble*	ehs-'tahr ehn oohn ah-pree-'eh-toh
Ya es tarde	*It's too late now*	yah ehs 'tahr-deh
Preocuparse por	*To worry about / To be concerned about or for*	preh-oh-kooh-'pahr-seh pohr

Disminuir el volumen	*To turn down the volume*	deehs-mee-nooh-'eehr ehl boh-'looh-men

Listen to Track 69

Disculpa pobre	*Lame excuse*	deehs-'koohl-pah 'poh-breh
Repetir de carretilla	*To rattle off or repeat mechanically*	rreh-peh-'teehr deh kah-rreh-'tee-yah
Ya voy	*I am coming*	yah 'boh-ee
En abonos	*On installments*	ehn ah-'bvoh-nohs
Me alegro mucho de verlo	*I'm very glad to see you.*	meh ah-'leh-groh 'mooh-choh deh 'behr-loh
De mal grado	*Reluctantly / Unwillingly*	deh mahl 'grah-doh
Debe de ser	*It must be / It probably is*	'deh-bveh deh sehr
A fin de cuentas	*After all / At the end of the day / In the end*	ah feehn deh kooh-'ehn-tahs
Al otro día	*On the following day*	ahl 'oh-troh 'dee-ah
¡Qué barbaridad!	*What nonsense! / What an atrocity!*	keh bahr-bvah-ree-'dad
Hacer teatro	*To be theatrical / To make a fuss / To exaggerate*	ah-'sehr teh-'ah-troh
Por lo pronto	*For now*	pohr loh 'prohn-toh
Por lo menos	*At least*	pohr loh 'meh-nohs

Listen to Track 70

Poner adelantado	*To set forward*	poh-'nehr ah-deh-lahn-'tah-doh
Prohibida la entrada	*No trespassing*	proh-ee-'bvee-dah lah ehn-'trah-dah
Pasar a mejor vida	*To die / To pass on to a better world*	pah-'sahr a meh-'hohr 'bee-dah
O si no	*Or else*	oh see noh
Cuerpo docente	*Faculty of a school*	kooh-'ehr-poh doh-'sehn-teh
A duras penas	*With great difficulty*	ah 'dooh-rahs 'peh-nahs
Al poco rato	*A short while later*	ahl 'poh-koh 'rrah-toh
Todo el mundo	*Everybody*	'toh-doh ehl 'moohn-doh
Sin novedad	*As usual / without any new developments or events / uneventful*	seen noh-bveh-'dahd
Más allá (de)	*Beyond*	mahs ah-'yah (deh)
Entre bastidores	*Behind the scenes / Off-stage*	'ehn-treh bahs-tee-'doh-rehs
En un soplo	*In a second / In a moment*	ehn oohn 'soh-ploh
Hasta más no poder	*To the limit/ utmost*	'ahs-tah mahs noh poh-'dehr

Listen to Track 71

No obstante	_Notwithstanding / Nevertheless_	noh ohbvs-'tahn-teh
Día hábil	_Weekday / Workday_	'dee-ah 'ah-bveehl
Lo expuesto	_What has been said_	loh ehks-pooh-'ehs-toh
Con el propósito de	_With the aim of_	kohn ehl proh-'poh-see-toh deh
A lo mejor	_Maybe / Perhaps_	ah loh meh-'hohr
De hecho	_In fact_	deh 'eh-choh
Creer que no	_To think not_	kreh-'ehr keh noh
Cerca de	_Near to / Close to_	'sehr-kah deh
Al instante	_Instantly / Straight away / At once_	ahl eehns-'tahn-teh
¿Qué le debo?	_How much do I owe you?_	keh leh 'deh-bvoh
Faltar a su palabra	_To break one's word_	fahl-'tahr ah sooh pah-'lah-bvrah
De una vez por todas	_Once and for all_	deh 'ooh-nah behs pohr 'toh-dahs

Listen to Track 72

Pase usted	_Come in / Go ahead_	'pah-seh oohs-'tehd
En tanto que	_While / As / For as long as_	ehn 'tahn-toh keh
Llevarse adelante	_To carry out / To be pursued / To be carried forward_	yeh-'bvahr-seh ah-deh-'lahn-teh

Ministerio de Relaciones Exteriores	*Foreign office*	mee-neehs-'teh-ree-oh deh rreh-lah-see-'oh-nehs ehks-teh-ree-'oh-rehs
Recibir noticias (de)	*To hear from*	rreh-see-'bveehr noh-'tee-see-ahs (deh)
De repuesto	*Spare / Extra*	deh rreh-pooh-'ehs-toh
Echar una cana al aire	*To go out for a good time or fling*	eh-'chahr 'ooh-nah 'kah-nah ahl 'a-ee-reh
Darle vuelta a la hoja	*To turn the page*	'dahr-leh booh-'ehl-tah ah lah 'oh-hah
¡Largo de aquí!	*Get out of here! / Get lost!*	'lahr-goh deh ah-'kee
A (or de) ciencia cierta	*With certainty / Definitely*	ah (deh) see-'ehn-see-ah see-'ehr-tah
Tener en mucho	*To esteem highly*	teh-'nehr ehn 'mooh-choh
De algún tiempo para acá	*For some time now*	deh ahl-'goohn tee-'ehm-poh 'pah-rah ah-'kah

Listen to Track 73

Más acá	*Closer*	mahs ah-'kah
Digno de	*Worthy of / Deserving of*	'deeg-noh deh
Hacer (un) alto	*To (make a) stop*	ah-'sehr (oohn) 'ahl-toh

De por sí	*By itself*	deh pohr see
Testigo de cargo	*Witness for the prosecution*	tehs-'tee-goh deh 'kahr-goh
A medio camino	*Halfway (to a place)*	ah 'meh-dee-oh kah-'meeh-noh
No hay que darle vueltas.	*There's no way around it.*	no 'a-ee keh 'dahr-leh booh-'ehl-tahs
A vista de	*In the presence of*	ah 'beehs-tah deh
Me repugna.	*It repels/disgusts me.*	meh rreh-'poohg-nah
A toda costa	*At all costs*	ah 'toh-dah 'kohs-tah
Ahora bien	*Now then / Well now / However*	ah-'oh-rah bee-'ehn
Días de antaño	*Old days*	'dee-ahs deh ahn-'tah-nyoh

Listen to Track 74

Por aquí	*This way / Over here*	pohr ah-'kee
Pasar el rato	*To pass time / Hangout / Spend time*	pah-'sahr ehl 'rrah-toh
Al revés	*In reverse / Backwards / In the opposite way*	ahl rreh-'bvehs
Hombre de estado	*Statesman*	'ohm-breh deh ehs-'tah-doh
Hacer un trato	*To make a deal*	ah-'sehr oohn 'trah-toh
Sala de recibo	*Reception room*	'sah-lah deh rreh-'see-bvoh

Certificado (or Fe, or Partida, or acta) de nacimiento	*Birth certificate*	sehr-tee-fee-'kah-doh (feh, pahr-'tee-dah, 'ahk-tah) deh nah-see-mee-'ehn-toh
Perder de vista	*To lose sight of*	pehr-'dehr deh 'beehs-tah
En el momento preciso	*On the right moment*	ehn ehl moh-'mehn-toh preh-'see-soh
Dar gusto (a alguien)	*To please (someone)*	dahr 'goohs-toh (ah 'ahl-gee-ehn)
Al (or en) rededor	*Around*	ahl-reh-deh-'dohr (ehn rreh-deh-'dohr)
Ondulado permanente	*Permanent wave*	ohn-dooh-'lah-doh pehr-mah-'nehn-teh

Listen to Track 75

Año entrante	*Next year*	'ah-nyoh ehn-'trahn-teh
Tener hambre	*To be hungry*	teh-'nehr 'ahm-breh
Si mal no recuerdo	*If I remember correctly*	see mahl noh rreh-kooh-'ehr-doh
Poner en ridículo	*To humiliate / Make a fool of*	poh-'nehr ehn rree-'dee-kooh-loh
Me hace falta.	*I need it.*	meh 'ah-seh 'fahl-tah

Con mucho gusto	*Gladly*	kohn 'mooh-choh 'goohs-toh
En concreto	*Concretely / To sum up*	ehn kohn-'kreh-toh
Ir a pie	*To walk / To go on foot*	eehr ah pee-'eh
A que	*I bet that... (not a real wager)*	ah keh
En (or a) ninguna parte	*Nowhere*	ehn (ah) neehn-'gooh-nah 'pahr-teh
Dar (or Darse) la vuelta	*To turn (to turn around)*	dahr ('dahr-seh) lah booh-'ehl-tah
Estar torcido con	*To be on unfriendly terms with*	ehs-'tahr tohr-'see-doh kohn

Listen to Track 76

En vez de	*Instead of*	ehn behs deh
Sacar punta a un lápiz	*To sharpen a pencil*	sah-'kahr 'poohn-tah ah oohn 'lah-peehs
¿Quién sabe?	*Who knows? (meaning I don't know)*	kee-'ehn 'sah-bveh
Hacer un viaje	*To make a trip / To go on a journey*	ah-'sehr oohn bee-'ah-heh
¿De parte de quién?	*Who is calling?*	deh 'pahr-teh deh kee-'ehn
Ir de compras	*To go shopping*	eehr deh 'kohm-prahs

Traer puesto	To wear / To have on	trah-'ehr pooh-'ehs-toh
Ha de ser verdad.	It must be true.	ah deh sehr behr-'dahd
Estar de turno	To be on duty	ehs-'tahr deh 'toohr-noh
Por regla general	As a general rule / Usually	pohr 'rreh-glah heh-neh-'rahl
Estar de vacaciones	To be on vacation	ehs-'tahr deh bah-kah-see-'oh-nehs
¿Hasta dónde?	How far?	'ahs-tah 'dohn-deh
Acerca de	About	ah-'sehr-kah deh

Listen to Track 77

Tener en la mente	To have in mind	teh-'nehr ehn lah 'mehn-teh
Hacer las maletas	To pack / To get ready to leave	ah-'sehr lahs mah-'leh-tahs
De subida	On the way up	deh sooh-'bvee-dah
Por el momento	For the moment	pohr ehl moh-'mehn-toh
Al mismo tiempo	At the same time	ahl 'meehs-moh tee-'ehm-poh
No poder más	To be exhausted / To be unable to take it anymore	noh poh-'dehr mahs
Obra maestra	Masterpiece	'oh-bvrah mah-'ehs-trah
Verse obligado a	To be obliged or forced to	'behr-seh oh-blee-'gah-doh ah

Algo por el estilo	*Similar / Sort of*	'ahl-goh pohr ehl ehs-'tee-loh
Formar parte de	*To be a part (or member) of*	fohr-'mahr 'pahr-teh deh
Dejarse de rodeos	*To stop the excuses*	deh-'hahr-seh deh 'rroh-deh-ohs
Hacer deducciones precipitadas	*To jump at conclusions*	ah-'sehr deh-doohk-see-'oh-nehs preh-see-pee-'tah-dahs
Estar salado	*To be unlucky*	ehs-'tahr sah-'lah-doh
Poner en duda	*To question / To doubt*	poh-'nehr ehn 'dooh-dah

Listen to Track 78

Por lo pronto	*For the time being*	pohr loh 'prohn-toh
Hasta la fecha	*Up to date / Up to now*	'ahs-tah lah 'feh-cha
Desde el principio	*All along / From the beginning*	'dehs-deh ehl preehn-'see-pee-oh
¿Qué hay de malo con eso?	*What's wrong with that?*	keh hay deh 'mah-loh kohn 'eh-soh
¿A cómo se vende?	*At what price?*	ah 'koh-moh seh 'behn-deh
Sírvase usted	*Help yourself*	'seehr-bvah-seh oohs-'tehd
De alguna manera	*Somehow*	deh ahl-'gooh-nah mah-'neh-rah

En cualquier caso	*In any case / Anyway*	ehn kooh-ˈahl-kee-ˈehr ˈkah-soh
Hasta aquí (or Hasta ahí)	*Up to now / So far*	ˈahs-tah ah-ˈkee (ˈahs-tah a-ˈee)
Ponerse en contra (de)	*To turn against*	poh-ˈnehr-seh ehn ˈkohn-trah (deh)
De un salto	*Quickly*	deh oohn ˈsahl-toh
De una tirada	*All at once*	deh ˈooh-nah tee-ˈrah-dah

Listen to Track 79

No cabe duda	*There is no doubt*	noh ˈkah-bveh ˈdooh-dah
Pasar un buen rato	*To have a good time*	pah-ˈsahr oohn booh-ˈehn ˈrrah-toh
Por (or En) consecuencia de	*Therefore / Consequently / In accordance with / Due to*	pohr (ehn) kohn-seh-kooh-ˈehn-see-ah deh
Estamos a mano	*We are even*	ehs-ˈtah-mohs ah ˈmah-noh
Cuanto antes	*As soon as possible*	kooh-ˈahn-toh ˈahn-tehs
Contra viento y marea	*Against all odds*	ˈkohn-trah bee-ˈehn-toh ee mah-ˈreh-ah
Prefiero que no	*I would rather not*	preh-fee-ˈeh-roh keh noh
Dar por sabido	*To take for granted*	dahr pohr sah-ˈbvee-doh

Estar fuera de la casa	To be out of the house / Away from home	ehs-'tahr fooh-'eh-rah deh lah 'kah-sah
Estar muy metido en	To be deeply involved in	ehs-'tahr 'mooh-ee meh-'tee-doh ehn
Nada en absoluto	Nothing at all	'nah-dah ehn ahbv-soh-'looh-toh
Si me hace el favor	If you would do me the favor	see meh 'ah-seh ehl fah-'bvohr

Listen to Track 80

Y así sucesivamente	And so on	ee ah-'see sooh-seh-see-bvah-'mehn-teh
Echarse una siesta	To take a nap	eh-'chahr-seh 'ooh-nah see-'ehs-tah
Poner en claro	To clear up / To clarify	poh-'nehr ehn 'klah-roh
Facilitar todos los datos	To furnish all the data	fah-see-lee-'tahr 'toh-dohs lohs 'dah-tohs
Tener probabilidad	To stand a chance	teh-'nehr proh-bvah-bvee-lee-'dahd
Estar de regreso	To be back	ehs-'tahr deh rreh-'greh-soh
Uno a la vez	One at a time	'ooh-noh ah lah behs
Hasta que se llene	Until full	'ahs-tah keh seh 'yeh-neh

Darse cuenta de (que)	To realize (that) / To notice	'dahr-seh kooh-'ehn-tah deh (keh)
¿Y qué?	So what?	ee keh
Aquí mismo	Right here	ah-'kee 'meehs-moh
Aquí cerca	Around here	ah-'kee 'sehr-kah

Listen to Track 81

Volver atrás	To go back	bohl-'bvehr ah-'trahs
Por instantes	At moments	pohr eehn-'stahn-tehs
Costar trabajo	To be very difficult	kohs-'tahr trah-'bvah-hoh
A pesar de que	Despite that	ah peh-'sahr deh keh
Unos pocos	A few	'ooh-nohs 'poh-kohs
Ir entendiendo	To begin to understand	eehr ehn-tehn-dee-'ehn-doh
¡No se preocupe!	Don't worry!	noh seh preh-oh-'kooh-peh
Déjeme salir	Let me out	'deh-heh-meh sah-'leehr
¿Adónde va?	Where are you going?	ah-'dohn-deh bah
¿Qué le parece?	What do you think of it? / How do you like it?	keh leh pah-'reh-seh?

Listen to Track 82

Si alguna vez	*If ever*	see ahl-ˈgooh-nah behs
Hacerse a un lado	*Step aside*	ah-ˈsehr-seh ah oohn ˈlah-doh
Una negativa terminante	*A flat denial*	ˈooh-nah neh-gah-ˈtee-bvah tehr-mee-ˈnahn-teh
¡A que no!	*I bet you didn't!*	ah keh noh
Quitarse un peso de encima	*To be relieved of*	kee-ˈtahr-seh oohn ˈpeh-soh deh ehn-ˈsee-mah
Tener cuidado (con)	*To be cautious (about) / To watch out (for)*	teh-ˈnehr kooh-eeh-ˈdah-doh (kohn)
¡Qué desgracia!	*How unfortunate!*	keh dehs-ˈgrah-see-ah
Ponerse de acuerdo	*To come to an agreement*	poh-ˈnehr-seh deh ah-kooh-ˈehr-doh
Poco a poco	*Gradually*	ˈpoh-koh ah ˈpoh-koh
No tiene importancia.	*It doesn't matter.*	noh tee-ˈeh-neh eehm-pohr-ˈtahn-see-ah
Caer en la cuenta	*To realize*	kah-ˈehr ehn lah kooh-ˈehn-tah
Por mi parte	*As far as I'm concerned*	pohr mee ˈpahr-teh
¿Cada cuánto tiempo?	*How often?*	ˈkah-dah kooh-ˈahn-toh tee-ˈehm-poh

Listen to Track 83

Suspender los pagos	_To stop payment_	soohs-pehn-'dehr lohs 'pah-gohs
Mañana por la tarde	_Tomorrow afternoon_	mah-'nyah-nah pohr lah 'tahr-deh
Aun cuando	_Even when_	ah-'oohn kooh-'ahn-doh
No tenga usted cuidado.	_Don't worry about it._	noh 'tehn-gah oohs-'tehd kooh-ee-'dah-doh
Sacar a uno de quicio	_To exasperate someone_	sah-'kahr ah 'uh-noh deh 'kee-see-oh
¡Qué horror!	_How awful!_	keh oh-'rrohr
De aquí para allá	_Back and forth_	deh ah-'kee 'pah-rah ah-'yah
Al pie de la letra	_Literally / By the book_	ahl pee-'eh deh lah 'leh-trah
¿Qué ventaja tiene?	_What is the use of it?_	keh behn-'tah-hah tee-'eh-neh?
Hacer frente (a)	_To face_	ah-'sehr 'frehn-teh (ah)
Se me pasó decirte.	_I forgot to tell you._	seh meh pah-'soh deh-'seehr-teh
Más vale tarde que nunca.	_Better late than never._	mahs 'bah-leh 'tahr-deh keh 'noohn-kah
¿Qué tiene de malo?	_What's wrong with it?_	keh tee-'eh-neh deh 'mah-loh
¿Para qué se usa?	_What is it used for?_	'pah-rah keh seh 'ooh-sah

¡Qué lástima!	*Too bad! / What a pity!*	keh 'lahs-tee-mah
Lo recién llegado	*A new arrival*	loh rreh-see-'ehn yeh-'gah-doh
Estar a cargo de	*To be in charge of*	ehs-'tahr a 'kahr-goh deh

PART 12: TIEMPO Y FRECUENCIA / TIME AND FREQUENCY

Listen to Track 84

Normalmente	*Normally*	nohr-mahl-'mehn-teh
Nunca	*Never*	'noohn-kah
Siempre	*Always*	see-'ehm-preh
A veces	*Sometimes*	ah beh-sehs
A menudo	*Often*	ah meh-'nooh-doh
Rara vez	*Rarely*	'rrah-rah behs
Cuando tengo tiempo	*When I have time*	kooh-'ahn-doh 'tehn-goh tee-'ehm-poh
Por la mañana	*In the morning*	pohr lah mah-'nyah-nah
Por la tarde	*In the afternoon/ evening*	pohr lah 'tahr-deh
Por la noche	*At night*	pohr lah 'noh-cheh
En mi tiempo libre	*In my free time*	ehn mee tee-'ehm-poh 'lee-bvreh
Los fines de semana	*At weekends*	lohs 'fee-nehs deh seh-'mah-nah
Durante la semana	*During the week*	duh-'rahn-teh lah seh-'mah-nah

CONCLUSION

Thank you for purchasing and for reading this book. Whether your intention was to learn basic Spanish phrases for everyday use or to properly navigate your travel escapades, I hope that this book was able to help you.

Spanish continues to be a very important language in the world, and learning it will open doors you never knew existed. To help you further in your Spanish language journey, the My Daily Spanish team would be happy to assist you in any way we can.

You can drop by the website mydailyspanish.com, where you can find all the resources you need to learn and embrace Spanish – fun articles, lifestyle topics, quizzes, and many other resources, all targeting different levels of learning.

You can also follow My Daily Spanish on social media, where we aim to give you fun and useful contents to help you keep learning Spanish daily.

- Facebook (facebook.com/mydailyspanish)
- Instagram (@holamydailyspanish)
- Twitter (@mydailyspanish)
- Pinterest (pinterest.com/mydailyspanish)

If you have any questions, requests, or concerns, do not hesitate to email support@mydailyspanish.com. It will be awesome to hear from you.

Gracias,

My Daily Spanish Team

HOW TO DOWNLOAD THE AUDIO?

Please take note that the audio files are in MP3 format and need to be accessed online. No worries though; it's quite easy!

On your computer, smartphone, iphone/ipad or tablet, simply go to this link:

https://mydailyspanish.com/phrasebook-audio

Did you have any problems downloading the audio? If so, feel free to send an email to support@mydailyspanish.com. We'll do our best to assist you, but we would greatly appreciate it if you could thoroughly review the instructions first.

Gracias,

My Daily Spanish Team

ABOUT MY DAILY SPANISH

MyDailySpanish.com is a website created to help busy learners learn Spanish. It is designed to provide a fun and fresh take on learning Spanish through:

- Helping you create a daily learning habit that you will stick to until you reach fluency, and
- Making learning Spanish as enjoyable as possible for people of all ages.

With the help of awesome content and tried-and-tested language learning methods, My Daily Spanish aims to be the best place on the web to learn Spanish.

The website is continuously updated with free resources and useful materials to help you learn Spanish. This includes grammar and vocabulary lessons plus culture topics to help you thrive in a Spanish-speaking location – perfect not only for those who wish to learn Spanish, but also for travelers planning to visit Spanish-speaking destinations.

For any questions, please email contact@mydailyspanish.com.

IMPROVE YOUR READING AND LISTENING SKILLS IN SPANISH

A COMPLETE AUDIO METHOD FOR SPANISH LANGUAGE LEARNING

- Four weeks of easy-to-follow daily audio lessons
- Practical dialogues based on real-life scenarios
- 1,000+ most frequently-used Spanish vocabulary
- Speaking practice, quizzes, and review lessons

LEARN MORE

https://geni.us/spanishlearning

Made in the USA
Middletown, DE
05 May 2022

65341896R00080